PICTURES WITH PINS

A Golden Hands book

Marshall Cavendish, London

Designs by:
James Alexander Nos. 25, 27, 28, 29, 31, 32, 36
Sue Blunden No. 40
Martin Coppard Nos. 4, 17, 18, 21, 24
Graham Elson Nos. 8, 15, 16, 19, 37
Bill Gutteridge No. 1
Paul Hutchinson and Jim Urquhart Nos. 41, 42, 43, 44
Edith Payne Nos. 2, 3, 5, 6, 7, 10, 11, 12, 13, 14, 22
Sonia Pitcher Nos. 26, 34, 35
Linda Proud Nos. 30, 33
Frank White Nos. 9, 20, 23, 38, 39

Photographs by:
Alan Duns
Graham Elson (Nos. 8, 15, 16, 19, 37)

Artwork by:
Bill Bayley

Edited by:
Vivien Bowler

The materials used in No's 2, 3, 5, 6, 7, 10, 11, 12, 13, 14 and 22 are available from Arts and Crafts, Norbury, London S.W.16

Published by Marshall Cavendish Publications Ltd, 58 Old Compton Street, London W1V 5PA

© Marshall Cavendish Publications Ltd, 58 Old Compton Street, London W1V 5PA

ISBN 0 85685 059 4

First printed June 1974
Second edition printed November 1974

Printed and bound by
Ben Johnson & Company Ltd, York

ABOUT THIS BOOK...

You don't have to be a dab hand with a paintbrush to create a picture these days. It's so much easier to do it with a hammer and nails and a reel of thread.

Thread sculpture is a new craft, but it's one of the simplest to learn as well as being most effective. Try it on a rainy afternoon, or (once you've hammered in the nails) while watching television in the evening.

It's great fun for children, too, and you'll be surprised how creative they can be in thinking up new designs. Under-twelves, however, may need some help with the hammering and stringing.

Starting with simple patterns, the book progresses to more intricate designs which you can follow exactly or use as the basis of your own ideas. The twelve signs of the Zodiac have been interpreted as thread sculpture designs which would make intriguing and unusual birthday gifts.

In addition to the nail and thread designs there is a special section on picture-making with nails alone. Each pattern is attractively illustrated and comes with clear step-by-step instructions.

This book could be the introduction to your most fascinating and enjoyable hobby.

CONTENTS

AN INTRODUCTION TO NAIL AND STRING ART

The art of making pictures from nails and string has greatly increased in popularity over the last few years. This is because while being a comparatively simple craft to master, striking results can be quickly achieved with both abstract and representational subjects. Once you have learnt the basic techniques, all you need is a good sense of colour and textures. These qualities will be required in order to select suitable nail or pins, string of the right colour or thickness, and an attractive covering for the board.

The main advantage of working with nails and string to produce works of art is that the materials are relatively inexpensive and easily available. It is also true to say that the techniques of passing and winding a length of string from one nail to another is not difficult to grasp. Thread sculptures, as they are called, can be either simple or elaborate and this does not necessarily depend on your level of expertise. All that matters is the intended image or impression and what is being depicted. However complicated a particular work may be there is no difference in the level of skill involved — only in the length of time and amount of materials taken up. You will find that the first eight patterns in the book are relatively simple in that they require either few nails or a very straight forward threading sequence.

To be an artistic and decorative success, a nail and string picture does not have to consist merely of one length of string joining a series of nails on a board to form a pattern. Two or more strings can be used — one on top of the other — to form a double image as for example in the Peacock design (page 78) or the Double Apollo (Page 79).

Choosing your materials

The board: It is very important to choose a board which will not buckle or warp and which will provide a good 'ground' for the nails. We recommend plywood or chipboard which is at least $\frac{1}{2}$in. (13mm.) thick, but a new board is not always necessary.

Providing the wood is not too pitted and scarred, an old piece of plywood should prove adequate. In fact; it is often true that an old panel will be better than a new one — as it will be less likely to warp. Old wood is dryer and more 'mature'. The wood size we recommend in each pattern is specially calculated to give an ample border to the design. If you can only obtain a small piece of wood reduce the size of the design accordingly.

The nails: Almost any type of nail will do, provided it has a head. This is to stop the string slipping off the nail as the pattern is worked. Panel pins are particularly suitable as are brass escutcheon pins. Where possible it is effective to try and match the colour of the nails to the colour of the thread, for example brass nails with gold thread, panel pins with silver thread and copper nails with copper coloured thread. Nails with small heads are preferable as they do not dominate the design at the expense of the string pattern. Ideally they should be $\frac{1}{2}$in. (13mm.) or $\frac{3}{4}$in. (19mm.) long.

The string: The colours and types of string used in our patterns are merely suggestions, experiment as much as possible to give your pictures flair and individuality. There is a great variety of suitable strings available. Apart from the familiar thin parcel cord, there are strings in a number of bright and attractive colours even silver, gold and copper. Nylon or corraleen strings can be bought at ironmongers and gardeners' supply shops. These are both ideal for nail and string work and cheap. In addition most of them have an attractive shine on the surface and by reflecting light they will give added appeal to the finished picture.

The wide choice of colours available makes raffia an excellent alternative to string. For really ambitious work, sisal cord is a good choice. Its hairy texture can produce some very unusual effects — especially if the sisal is dyed — but it is only suitable for large scale work.

There may be some difficulty in getting hold of a sufficient quantity of string of the right type. If this is the case, a very good alternative is wool. Odd skeins or balls can often be obtained at greatly reduced prices. This is an important factor because of the amount of thread necessary to make a nail and string pictures.

When using wool, choose colours that contrast well with each other. White wool is excellent as it helps to highlight other colours and give 'body' to the finished picture.

Making up a thread sculpture

Covering the board: There are two ways of treating the board; the first and the simplest, is to paint it and the second is to cover it with a fabric such as felt or hessian. If you decide to paint your board it is important to choose the kind of paint that gives a tough finish. A polyurethane based matt finish is undoubtedly the best. If you prefer to cover the board with fabric here are two ways in which it can be done.

Felt: The felt should be at least 2in. larger than the board and it should be pressed to remove any creases. Place the board in the centre of the felt and spread clear household adhesive along one edge of the board and fold the felt over it. Do the same on the opposite edge, pulling the felt taught. Mitre the corners (see diagram) then glue down the remaining edges.

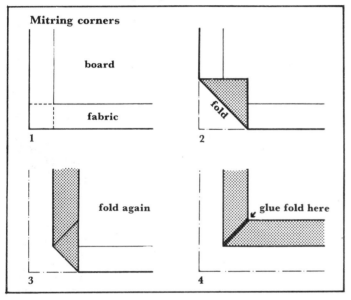

Hessian: The hessian should be at least 3in. larger than the board to allow for a hem. Press out all creases, turn in a $\frac{1}{4}$in. hem all round and press. Place the board in the centre of the hessian and fold the hessian over one side of the board. Secure in position with tacks at about $1\frac{1}{2}$in. intervals. Bring the opposite edge over the wood, pulling the hessian as taut as possible, and secure with tacks in the same way. Mitre the corners and secure the remaining edges with tacks.

Making the pattern: Our diagrams are all on squared grids and each square represents 1in. (25mm.). Buy, or rule out for yourself, some 1in. squared graph paper and then transfer the lines of dots exactly on to the graph paper. Mark in the letters as well as the numbers. Place the graph paper over the right side of the board, holding the corners in place with drawing pins.

Nailing the board: Hammer the nails in position through the paper using a depth gauge — a piece of wood or metal — to ensure they are all the same height (see diagram).

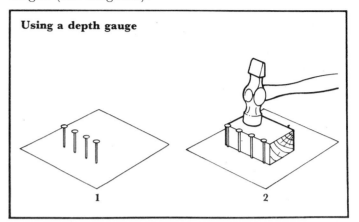

Threading the design: It is important to get string in long lengths. This will make threading easier and the fewer joins that have to be made in string of any one colour the better. Joining one piece of string to another should be done carefully. Whenever possible the join should be made at a nail. This will mean that in the finished picture the total impression will not be marred by unsightly knots. Knot the two lengths of string together, making sure that no slack is allowed to occur. Clip the ends of the strings as close to the knot as is possible without breaking or weakening it. Whenever you tie on or off place a spot of glue on the knot to make it more secure. When you pass the thread from one nail to another twist it once round the nail so that it does not slip off (see diagram). This does not apply to designs where the pattern is made by passing the thread round two nails at a time, for example Madonna on page 10. In such cases try to keep the thread as tight as possible and continue with an even rhythm until a tie off point.

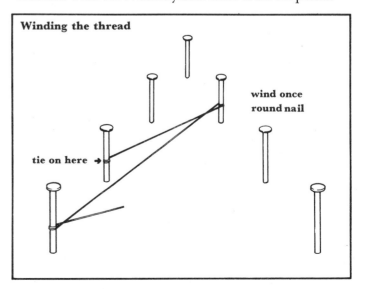

1
FULL
MOON

4
STARBURST

5
COMET

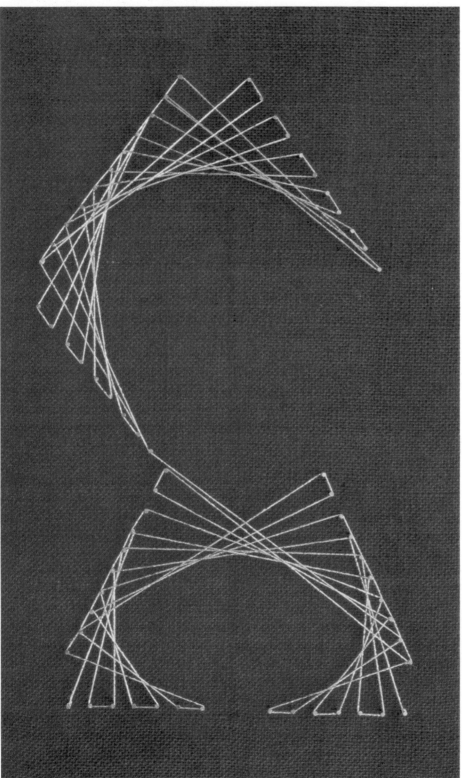

TROUT

6
SHEPHERD

14

8
WHIRLPOOL

You will need A piece of plywood or chipboard measuring 24in. (610mm.) square and at least ½in. (13mm.) thick; a piece of hessian large enough to cover the board plus 2in. (51mm.) all round; 1in. (25mm.) squared graph paper; 86 nails; clear household adhesive; a ball of gold thread and one of silver.

The design On 1in. squared graph paper make an actual size plan from the diagram using a dot to represent each nail. Make sure you space the dots evenly — a pair if dividers could be useful for this. Mark dots 1, 30 and 59.

The board Make up the board as described in the introduction.

Positioning the nails Place the graph paper over the right side of the board, holding the corners in place with drawing pins. Hammer the nails in position through the paper, and remove the paper pattern carefully.

Threading the design Tie the thread to 1 and pass to 30, 30 to 59, 59 to 2, 2 to 31, 31 to 60, 60 to 3, 3 to 32, 32 to 61, 61 to 4 and so on in this sequence until you return to 1. Vary the silver and gold thread as you wish always tying on and off at a nail. To give the design more body work a second layer of thread on top of the first.

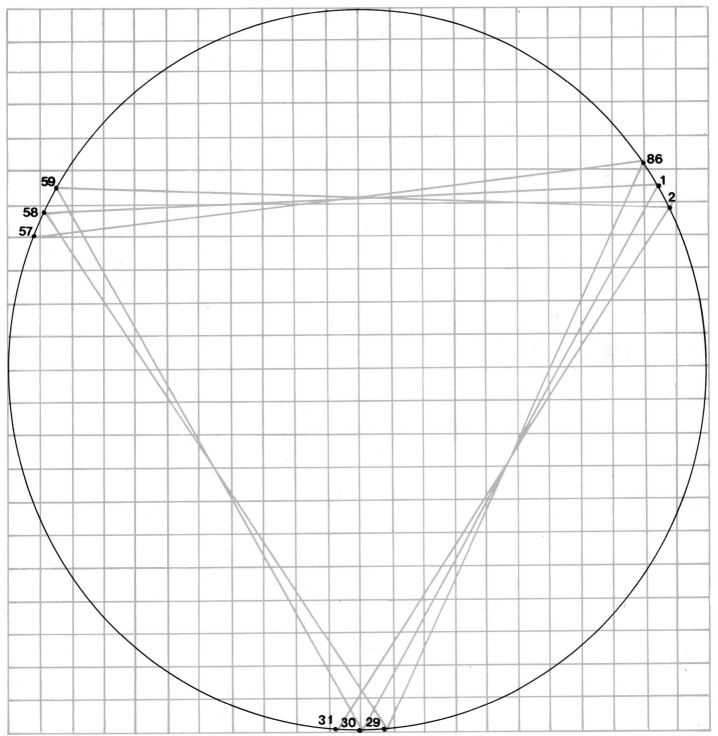

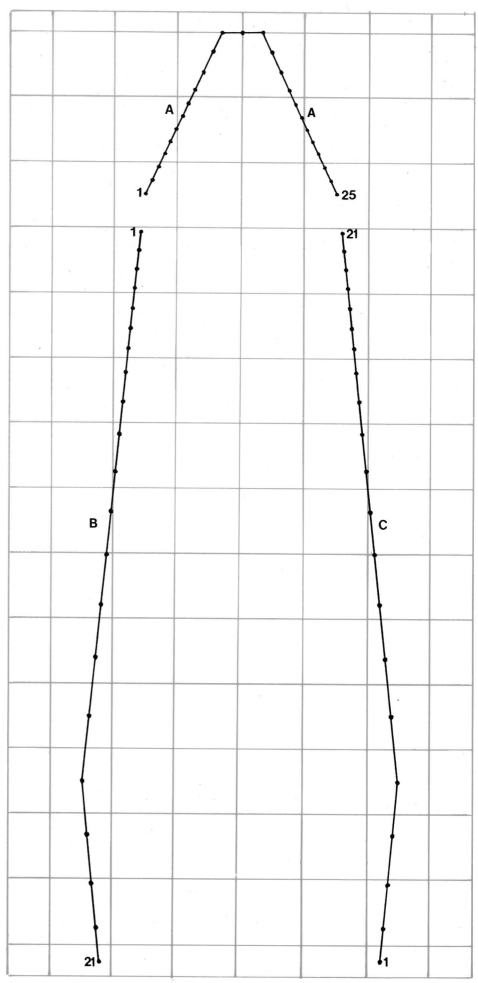

2 MADONNA

You will need A piece of plywood or chipboard measuring 18in. (457mm.) by 9in. (229mm.) and at least ½in. (13mm.) thick; a piece of hessian 21in. (533mm.) by 12in. (305mm.); about two dozen tacks; 1in. (25mm.) squared graph paper; 67 nails ½in. long and a ball of gold thread.

The design On 1in. squared graph paper make an actual size plan from the diagram, using a dot to represent each nail. Mark each line A1-A25, B1-B21 etc. spacing the dots exactly as shown.

The board Make up the board as described in the introduction.

Positioning the nails Place the graph paper over the right side of the board, holding the corners in place with drawing pins. Hammer the nails in position through the paper. Then carefully remove the graph paper.

Threading the design Tie the thread to A1 and pass it to A13, A13 to A14, A14 to A2, A2 to A3, A3 to A15, A15 to A16, A16 to A4, A4 to A5 and so on until you reach A24. From A24 pass the thread up to A12, A12 to A13, A13 to A25 and tie off. Tie on again at B1 and pass to C1, C1 to C2, C2 to B2, B2 to B3, B3 to C3, C3 to C4 and so on until you reach C21 and tie off.

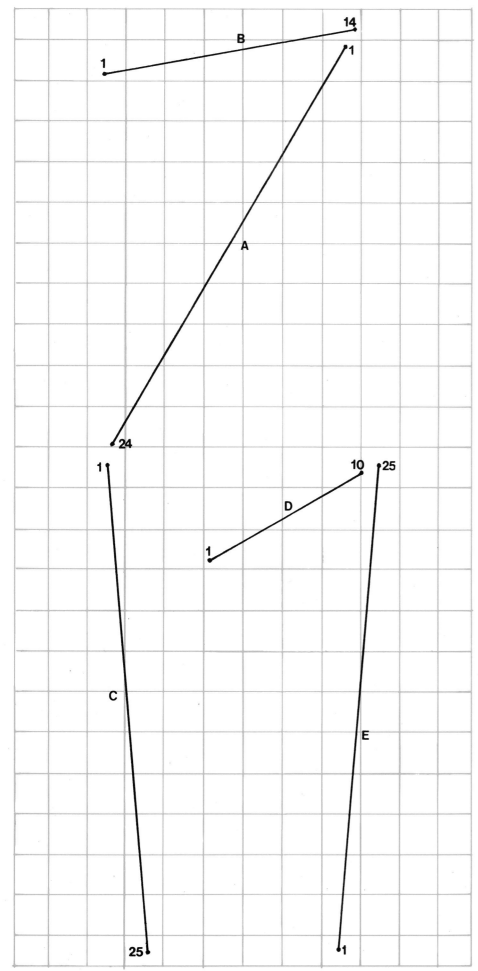

3
HERON

You will need A piece of plywood or chipboard measuring 27in. (686mm.) by 10in. (254mm.) and at least ½in. (13mm.) thick; a piece of hessian 30in. (762mm.) by 13in. (330mm.); 1in. (25mm.) squared graph paper; 95 nails ½in. long and a ball of black thread.

The design On 1in. squared graph paper make an actual size plan from the diagram using a dot to represent each nail. Mark each line A1-A24, B1-14 etc. spacing the dots evenly along each line.

The board Make up the board as described in the introduction.

Positioning the nails Place the graph paper over the right side of the board, holding the corners in place with drawing pins. Hammer the nails in position through the paper. Then carefully remove the graph paper.

Threading the design Tie the thread to A1, A1 to B1, B1 to B2, B2 to A2, A2 to A3, A3 to B3, B3 to B4 and so on until you reach B14. From B14 pass the thread to C1, C1 to C2, C2 to A1, A1 to A2, A2 to C3, C3 to C4, C4 to A3, A3 to A4 and so on until you reach C25. From C25 pass the thread up the right side of line C to C1, C1 to E1, E1 to E2, E2 to C2, C2 to C3, C3 to E3, E3 to E4 and so on until you reach E25. From E25 pass the thread to E24, E24 to D1, D1 to E23, E23 to E22, E22 to D2, D2 to D3, D3 to E21, E21 to E20, E20 to D4, D4 to D5, D5 to E19, E19 to E18, E18 to D6, D6 to D7 and so on until you reach E25 and tie off.

4 STARBURST

You will need A piece of plywood or chipboard measuring 20in. (508mm.) by 14in. (356mm.) and at least ½in. (13mm.) thick; a small tin of white paint; a paint brush; 1in.(25mm.) squared graph paper; 126 nails ½in. long and three different coloured reels of thread — we used orange, red and white.

The design On 1in. squared graph paper make an actual size plan from the diagram using a dot to represent each nail. The dots should be spaced evenly in both diamonds.

The board Make up the board as described in the introduction.

Positioning the nails Place the graph paper over the right side of the board, holding the corners in place with drawing pins. Hammer the nails in position through the paper, and remove the paper pattern carefully.

Threading the design Tie on with orange thread at A1 and pass it to A33, wind the thread clockwise round A33 and pass to A2, A2 to A34, A34 to A3, A3 to A35 and so on until you return to A1 (which is also B1). From B1 pass the thread to B33, B33 to B2, B2 to B34, B34 to B3 and so on until you return to B1 and tie off. Tie on again with red at. A17 and pass the thread to A49, A49 to A18, A18 to A50 and so on until you return to A17 (which is also B49). From B49 pass the thread to B17, B17 to B50, B50 to B18 and so on until you return to B49 and tie off. Tie on again with white at A57 and pass the thread to A25, A25 to A58, A58 to A26 and so on until you return to A25 and tie off. Repeat this sequence tying on at B9.

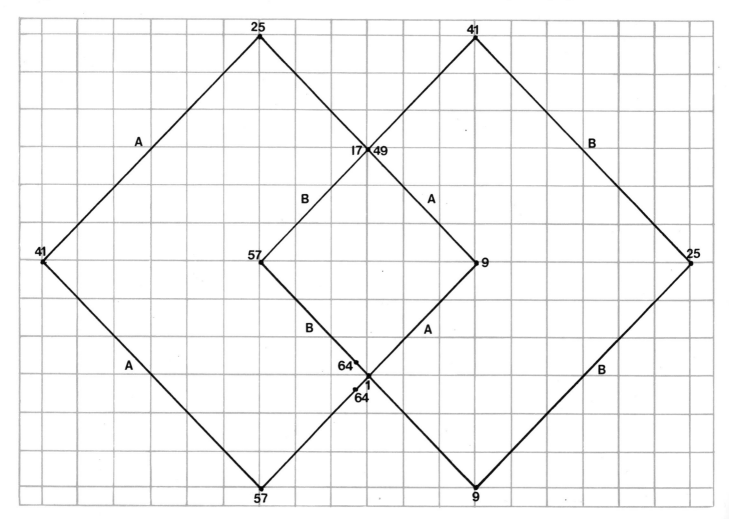

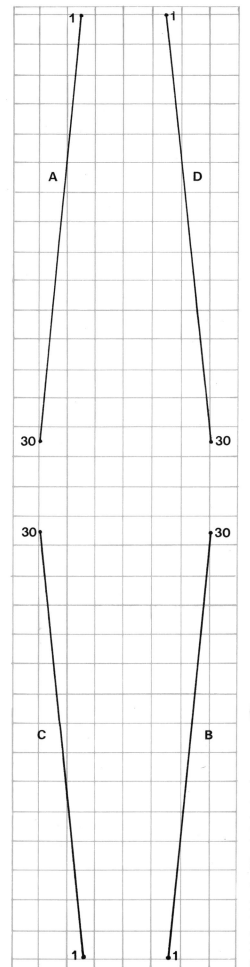

5
COMET

You will need A piece of plywood or chipboard measuring 36in. (915mm.) by 8in. (203mm.) and at least ½in. (13mm.) thick; a piece of hessian 39in. (991mm.) by 11in. (279mm.); 1in. (25mm.) squared graph paper; 120 nails ½in. long and one ball of copper coloured thread.
The design On 1in. squared graph paper make an actual size plan from the diagram using a dot to represent each nail. Mark each line A1-A30, B1-B30 etc. as shown on the diagram, and space the dots evenly along each line.

The board Make up the board as described in the introduction.
Positioning the nails Place the graph paper over the right side of the board, holding the corners in place with drawing pins. Hammer the nails in position through the paper, and remove the paper pattern carefully.
Threading the design Tie the thread to A1 and pass to B1, B1 to B2, B2 to A2, A2 to A3, A3 to B3, B3 to B4, B4 to A4 and so on until you reach A30. From A30 pass the thread to A29, A29 to D1, D1 to D2, D2 to A28, A28 to A27, A27 to D3, D3 to D4 and so on until you reach D29. From D29 pass the thread to D30 and from D30 to C30. C30 to C29, C29 to D29, D29 to D28, D28 to C28, C28 to C27, C27 to D27 and so on until you reach D1. From D1 pass the thread down to C1 again and thence to B29, B29 to B28, B28 to C2, C2 to C3, C3 to B27, B27 to B26, B26 to C4, C4 to C5 and so on until you reach C29. From C29 pass the thread back to B1 and tie off.

6
SHEPHERD

You will need A piece of plywood or chipboard measuring 18in. (457mm.) by 11in. (279mm.) and at least ½in. (13mm.) thick; a piece of hessian 21in. (533mm.) by 14in. (356mm.); 1in. (25mm.) squared graph paper; 65 nails ½in. long and a ball of silver thread.

The design On 1in. squared graph paper make an actual size plan using a dot to represent each nail. Mark each line A1-A11, B1-B11, C1-C19 etc. as shown on the diagram, spacing the dots evenly along each line.

The board Make up the board as described in the introduction.

Positioning the nails Place the graph paper over the right side of the board, holding the corners in place with drawing pins. Hammer the nails in position through the paper, and remove the paper pattern carefully.

Threading the design Tie the thread to D1 and pass to F7, F7 to F6, F6 to D2, D2 to D3, D3 to F5, F5 to F4 and so on until you reach F1 and tie off. Tie the thread to E1. From E1 pass the thread to C7, C7 to C6, C6 to E2, E2 to E3, E3 to C5, C5 to C4 and so on until you reach C1. Pass the thread to C2, C2 to D10, D10 to D9, D9 to C3, C3 to C4, C4 to D8 and so on until you reach C10. From C10 pass the thread to D1, D1 to D2, D2 to C11, C11 to A2, A2 to A1, A1 to C12, C12 to C13, C13 to A3, A3 to A4, A4 to C14, C14 to C15, C15 to A5, A5 to A6 and so on until you reach A10. From A10 pass the thread to B11, B11 to A11, A11 to A10, A10 to B10, B10 to B9, B9 to A9, A9 to A8, A8 to B8, B8 to B7, B7 to A7, A7 to A6, A6 to B6 and so on until you reach A1 and tie off.

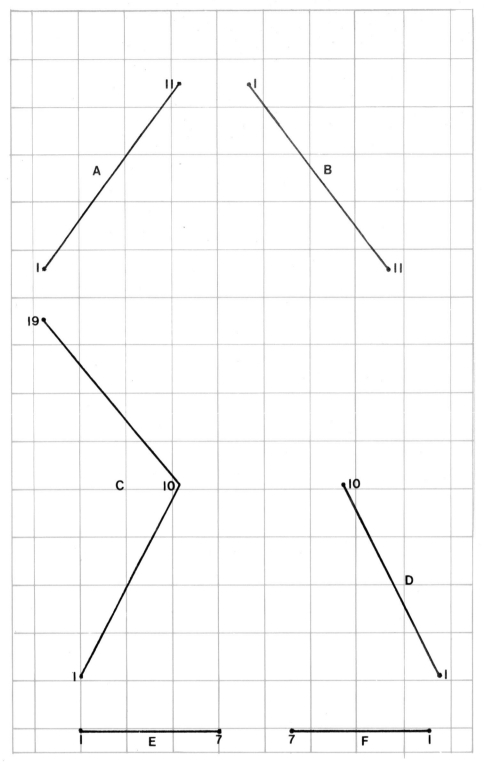

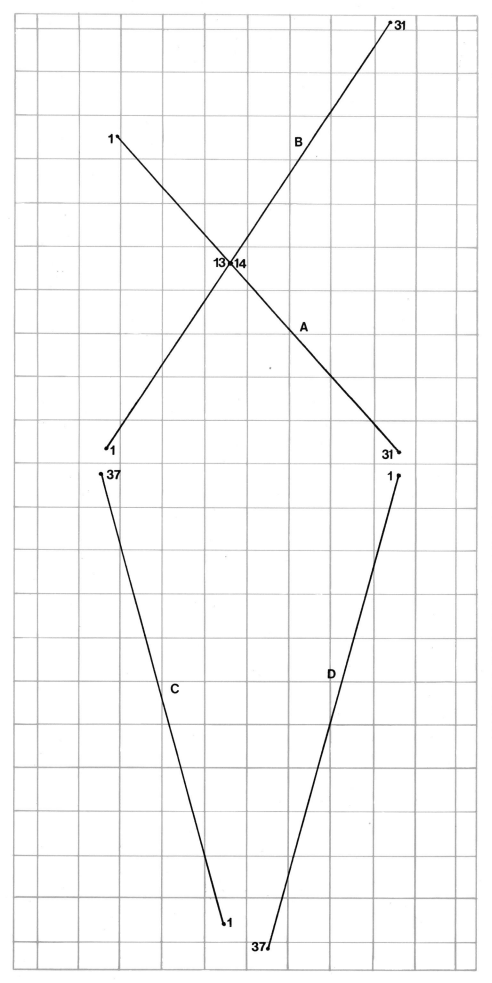

7

TROUT

You will need A piece of plywood or chipboard measuring 27in. (686mm.) by 10in. (254mm.) and at least ½in. (13mm.) thick; a piece of hessian 30in. (762mm.) by 13in. (330mm.); 1in. (25mm.) squared graph paper; 135 nails ½in. long and a ball of black thread.

The design On 1in. squared graph paper make an actual size plan from the diagram using a dot to represent each nail. Mark each line A1-A32, B1-B31 etc. spacing the dots evenly along each line.

The board Make up the board as described in the introduction.

Positioning the nails Place the graph paper over the right side of the board, holding the corners in place with drawing pins. Hammer the nails in position through the paper. Then carefully remove the graph paper.

Threading the design Tie the thread to A1 and pass to B15, B15 to B16, B16 to A2, A2 to A3, A3 to B17, B17 to B18 B18 to A4, A4 to A5 and so on until you reach B28. Take the thread to A13 and tie off. Tie on again at C7 and pass to B1, B1 to B2, B2 to C8, C8 to C9, C9 to B3, B3 to B4, B4 to C10, C10 to C11 and so on until you reach B31 from C37 and tie off. Tie on. again at D32 and pass to A31, A31 to A30, A30 to D31, D31 to D30, D30 to A29, A29 to A28 and so on until you reach A1 from D1 and tie off. Tie on again at C25 and pass the thread to D37, D37 to D36, D36 to C24, C24 to C23, C23 to D35, D35 to D34 and so on until you reach D13 and tie off.

You will need A piece of plywood or chipboard measuring 20¼in. (514mm.) by 18½in. (460mm.) and at least ½in. (13 mm.) thick; a piece of felt large enough to cover the board plus 2in. (51mm.) all round; 1in. (25mm.) squared graph paper; about 321 panel pins; one large headed nail; clear household adhesive and a ball of coloured cotton.

The design On 1in. squared graph paper make an actual size plan from the diagram, using a dot to represent each nail. Draw a line from the centre point A to the beginning of the spiral then draw a second line a few degrees round from this to the second ring on the spiral and with a dot mark the nail position. Continue spacing the nails evenly as shown on the diagram until the end of the spiral is reached. Make sure that the lines do not touch each other.

The board Make up the board as described in the introduction.

Positioning the nails Place the graph paper over the right side of the board, holding the corners in place with drawing pins. Hammer the nails in position through the paper. At point A use a large headed nail instead of a panel pin. Then carefully remove the graph paper.

Threading the design Tie the thread to pin 1 and pass round A to pin 2, back to A then to pin 3, to A to pin 4 etc. Continue in numerical sequence passing the thread round A each time, finally tying off at the end of the spiral.

8
WHIRLPOOL

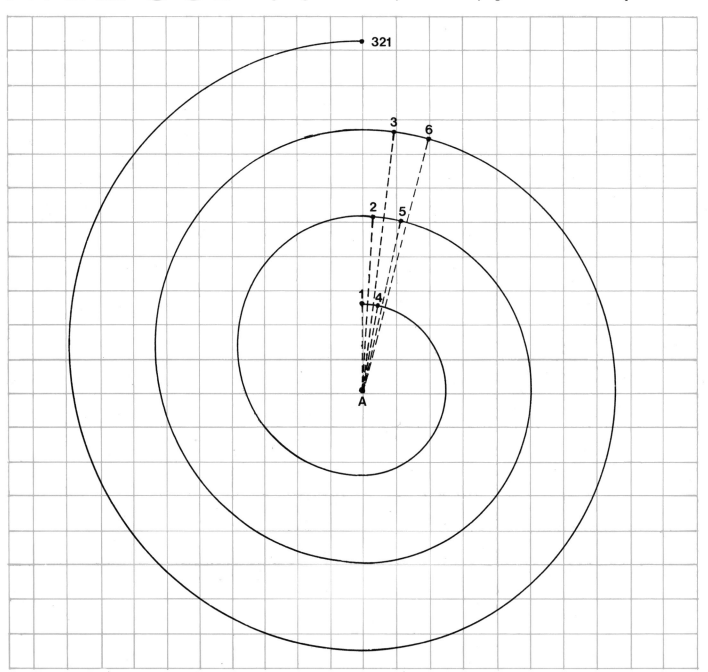

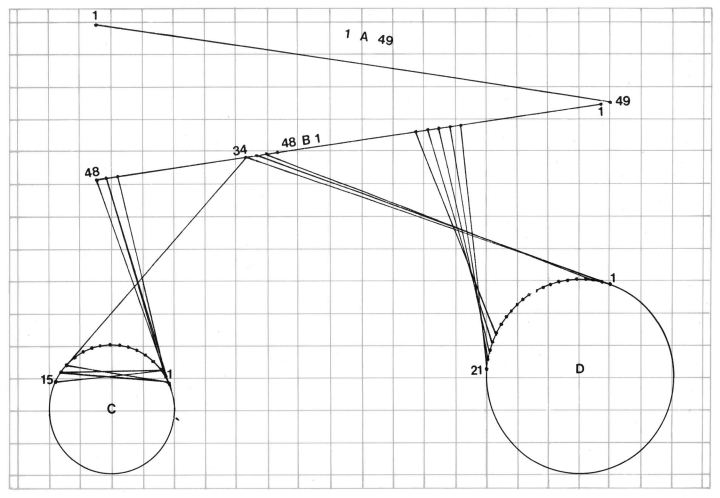

9 MOON BUGGY

You will need A piece of plywood or chipboard measuring 24in. (610mm.) by 16in. (406mm.) and at least ½in. (13 mm.) thick; a small tin of matt black paint; a paint brush; 1in. (25mm.) squared graph paper; 205 nails ¾in. (19mm.) long and a ball of red thread.

The design On 1in. squared graph paper make an actual size plan from the diagram using a dot to represent each nail. Mark each line A1-49, B1-48 etc. spacing the dots evenly along each line.

The board Paint the board with matt black paint and leave until quite dry.

Positioning the nails Place the graph paper over the right side of the board, holding the corners in place with drawing pins. Hammer the nails in position through the paper and then remove the paper carefully.

Threading the design Tie the thread to A1 and pass to A49 inside the line A, A49 to A2, A2 to B1, B1 to A3, A3 to B2 and so on until you reach B48. From B48 pass the thread to C1, from C1 to B47, B47 to C2 and so on until you reach C15. From C15 pass the thread to C1, C1 to C16, C16 to C2 until you return to C15. From C15 pass the thread to B34, B34 to D1, D1 to B33, B33 to D2 until you reach D21. From D21 pass the thread to D1, D1 to D22, D22 to D2 until you return to D21 and tie off.

10
PASSER BY

You will need A piece of plywood or chipboard measuring 18in. (457mm.) by 11in. (279mm.) and at least ½in. (13 mm.) thick; a piece of hessian 21in. (533mm.) by 14in. (356mm.); about two dozen tacks; 1in. (25mm.) squared graph paper; 152 nails ½in. long and a ball of gold thread.

The design On 1in. squared graph paper make an actual size plan from the diagram using a dot to represent each nail. Mark each line A1-A22, B1-B13 etc. spacing the exact number of dots evenly along each line.

The board Make up the board as described in the introduction.

Positioning the nails Place the graph paper over the right side of the board, holding the corners in place with drawing pins. Hammer the nails in position through the paper. Then carefully remove the graph paper.

Threading the design Tie the thread to A1 and pass to B1, B1 to B2, B2 to A2, A2 to A3, A3 to B3, B3 to B4, B4 to A4, A4 to A5 and so on until you reach A13. From A13 pass the thread down the right side of line A to B13. From B13 pass the thread to C1, C1 to C2, C2 to A1, A1 to A2, A2 to A3, C3 to C4 and so on until you reach A22. From A22 pass the thread to C22 and tie off. Tie on again at E1 and pass the thread to D1, D1 to D2, D2 to E2, E2 to E3, E3 to D3, D3 to D4 and so on until you reach E13. From E13 pass the thread down the right side of line E to D13 and up the left side to F1, F1 to F2, F2 to E1, E1 to E2, E2 to F3, F3 to F4 and so on until you reach E22. From E22 pass the thread up the left side of line F and F22, F22 to F8, F8 to F9, F9 to H1, J1 to H2, H2 to F10, F10 to F11, F11 to H3, H3 to H4 and so on until you get to F21. From F21 pass the thread to J1, J1 to J2, J2 to H12, H12 to H11, H11 to J3, J3 to J4 and so on until you reach H1. From H1 pass the thread to G1, G1 to G2, G2 to H2, H2 to H3, H3 to G3, G3 to G4 and so on until you reach G12. From G12 pass the thread to H12 and tie off.

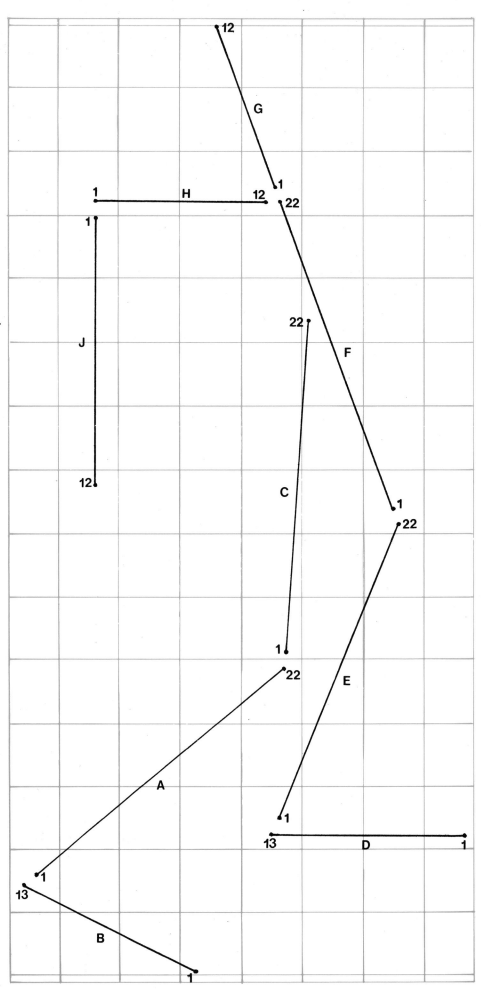

26

11 PLAYMATE

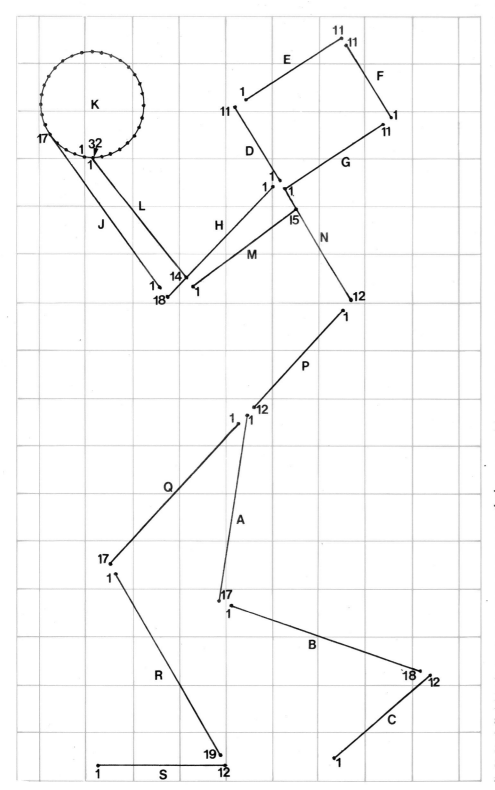

You will need A piece of plywood or chipboard measuring 18in. (457mm.) by 10in. (254mm.) and at least ½in. (13 mm.) thick; a piece of hessian 21in. (533mm.) by 13in. (330mm.); 1in. (25mm.) squared graph paper; 207 nails ½in. long; about two dozen tacks and a ball of thread.

The design On 1in. squared graph paper make an actual size plan from the diagram using a dot to represent each nail. Mark each line A1-A17, B1-B18 etc. spacing the exact number of dots evenly along each line.

The board Make up the board as described in the introduction.

Positioning the nails Place the graph paper over the right side of the board, holding the corners in place with drawing pins. Hammer the nails in position through the paper. Then carefully remove the graph paper.

Threading the design Tie the thread to A1 and pass to B1, B1 to B2, B2 to A2, A2 to A3, A3 to B3, B3 to B4 and so on until you reach B18. From B18 pass the thread to C1, C1 to C2, C2 to B17, B17 to B16, B16 to C3, C3 to C4 and so on until you reach C12. From C12 pass the thread to B7 and tie off. Tie on again at G1 and pass the thread to D1, D1 to E1, E1 to E2, E2 to D2, D2 to D3 and so on until you reach D11. Take the thread round E11 to G10, G10 to G11, G11 to F11, F11 to F10, F10 to G9, G9 to G8, G8 to F9 and so on until you reach F1. From F1 take the thread to G1. From G1 pass the thread to D1, D1 to J1, J1 to J2, J2 to H1, H1 to H2, H2 to J3, J3 to J4, J4 to H3, H3 to H4 and so on until you reach H18. From H18 pass the thread up to K1 and twist round once, K1 to K12, K12 to K23, K23 to K2, K2 to K13, K13 to K24, K24 to K3, K3 to K14 and so on until you reach K32 (which is also L1). From L1 pass the thread to M1, M1 to M2, M2 to L2, L2 to L3 and so on until you reach M15 (which is also N3). From N3 pass the thread round N2 and N1 and on to P1, P1 to P2, P2 to N3, N3 to N4, N4 to P3 and so on until you reach P12. From P12 take the thread to Q1, Q1 to R1, R1 to R2, R2 to Q2, Q2 to Q3 and so on until you reach R16. From R16 take the thread down to R19, R19 to S1, S1 to S2, S2 to R18, R18 to R17, R17 to S3, S3 to S4 and so on until you reach R9 and tie off.

27

12 BALLERINA

From I8 pass the thread down the left side of line J to K19, K19 to J15, J15 to K5, K5 to K7, K7 to J14, J14 to J13, J13 to K9, K9 to K11, and so on until you reach J5 and tie off. Tie on again at X and pass the thread to H17, H17 to H16, H16 to L16, L16 to L15, L15 to H15 and so on until you reach L1. From

L1 return the thread to X, X to N11, N11 to M1, M1 to M2, M2 to N10, N10 to N9, and so on until you complete the section. Thread sections NO and CO in the same way and tie off. Tie on again at L16 and pass the thread to K16, K16 to K15, K15 to L15, L15 to L14, and so on until you reach L1 and tie off.

You will need A piece of plywood or chipboard measuring 18in. (457mm.) by 10in. (254mm.) and at least ½in. (13 mm.) thick; a piece of hessian 21in. (533mm.) by 13in. (330mm.); 1in. (25mm.) squared graph paper; 227 nails ½in. long; and two balls of thread of different colours.

The design On 1in. squared graph paper make an actual size plan from the diagram using a dot to represent each nail. Mark each line A1-A21, B1-B9 etc. spacing the dots evenly except for those in lines D, E, G, H, J and K where you should reproduce the dots eactly as shown on the diagram.

The board Make up the board a described in the introduction.

Positioning the nails Place the graph paper over the right side of the board, holding the corners in place with drawing pins. Hammer the nails in position through the paper. Then carefully remove the graph paper.

Threading the design Tie the thread to A1 and pass to B1, B1 to B2, B2 to A2, A2 to A3, A3 to B3, B3 to B4, B4 to A4, and so on until you reach A8. From A8 take the thread down the left side of line A round B9 and up to C1, C1 to C2, C2 to A2, A2 to A3, A3 to C3, C3 to C4 and so on until you reach A20. From A20 take the thread up the right side of C to X, the centre point. From X take the thread round D2, D2 to D1, D1 to D3, D3 to D2, D2 to D4, D4 to E1, E1 to E2, E2 to D5, D5 to D6, D6 to E3 and so on until you reach D15. From D15 pass the thread down the left side of line E to E17, E17 to F1, F1 to F2, F2 to E16, E16 to E15, E15 to F3, F3 to F4 and so on until you reach E10 and tie off. Tie on again at H15 and pass the thread to G1, G1 to G2, G2 to H18, H18 to H19, H19 to G3, G3 to G4, G4 to H20 and so on until you reach G11. From G11 pass the thread round G14 and up to J1, J1 to I1, I1 to I2, I2 to J2, J2 to J3 (which is also G10), J3 to I3 and so on until you reach I8.

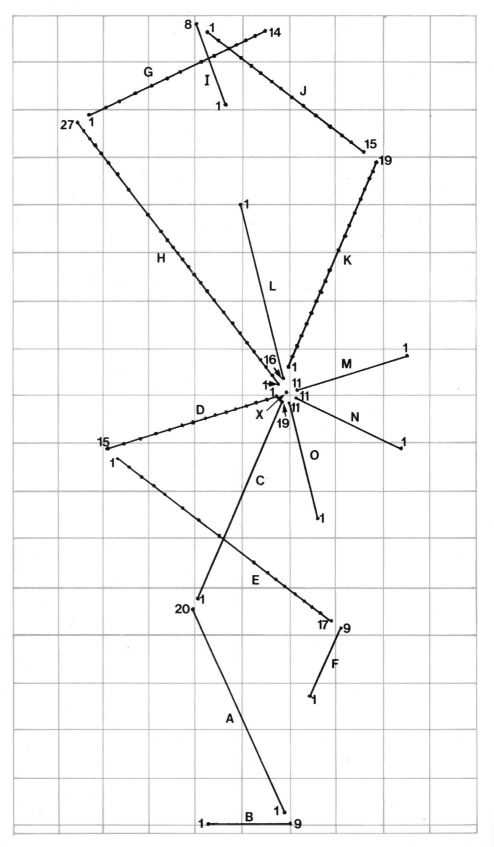

13 ACROBAT

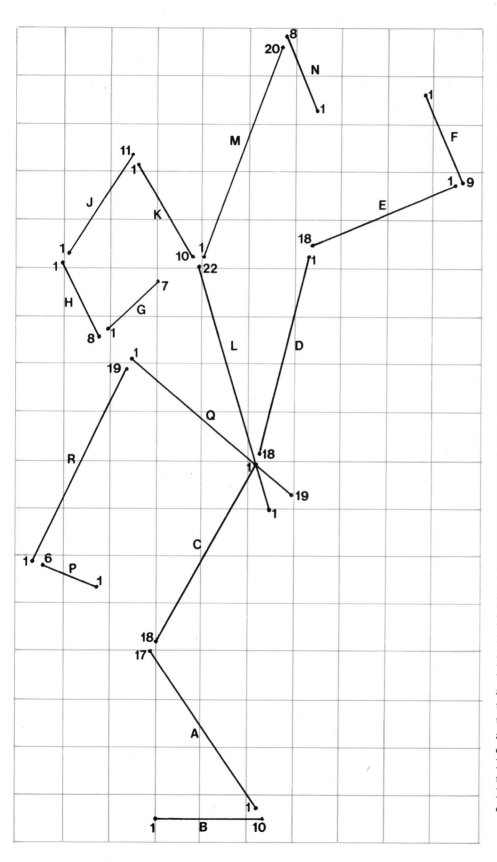

You will need A piece of plywood or chipboard measuring 18in. (457mm.) by 11in. (279mm.) and at least ½in. (13 mm.) thick; a piece of hessian 21in. (533mm.) by 14in. (356mm.); 1in. (25mm.) squared graph paper; 218 nails ½in. long; about two dozen tacks and two balls of different coloured thread.

The design On 1in. squared graph paper make an actual size plan from the diagram using a dot to represent each nail. Mark each line A1–A17, B1–B10 etc. spacing the dots evenly along the line.

The board Make up the board as described in the introduction.

Positioning the nails Place the graph paper over the right side of the board, holding the corners in place with drawing pins. Hammer the nails in position through the paper. Then carefully remove the graph paper.

Threading the design Tie the thread to A1 and pass to B1, B1 to A2, A2 to A3, A3 to B2, B2 to B3, B3 to A4, A4 to A5, A5 to B4, B4 to B5 and so on until you reach A11. From A11 pass the thread to A10 and down line A to A1. Take the thread round A1 to B10, B10 to C18, C18 to C17, C17 to A1, A1 to A2, A2 to C16, C16 to C15, C15 to A3, A3 to A4, A4 to C14, C14 to C13 and so on until you reach C1. Pass the thread to D18, D18 to E17, E17 to E16, E16 to D17, D17 to D16, D16 to E15, E15 to E14 and so on until you reach D2. From D2 take the thread to E1, E1 to F9, F9 to D1, D1 to E18, E18 to E1. From E1 take the thread to F1, F1 to E2, E2 to E3, E3 to F2, F2 to F3, F3 to E4, E4 to E5 and so on until you reach E10 and tie off. Tie on again at H7 and pass the thread to G7, G7 to G6, G6 to H6, H6 to H5, H5 to G5, G5 to G4, G4 to H4, H4 to H3, H3 to G3, G3 to G2, G2 to H2, H2 to H1, H1 to G1, G1 to H8, H8 to H1, H1 to J1, J1 to K1, K1 to K2, K2 to J2, J2 to J3 and so on until you reach J11. From J11 pass the thread round L22 and up to M1, M1 to L1, L1 to L2, L2 to M2, M2 to M3, M3 to L3, L3 to L4 and so on until you reach L22. From L22 take the thread up to M20, M20 to N1, N1 to M19, M19 to M18, M18 to N2, N2 to N3, N3 to M17, M17 to M16, M16 to N4, N4 to N5, N5 to M15, M15 to M14, M14 to N6, N6 to N7, N7 to M13, M13 to M12, M12 to N8 and tie off. Tie on again at R2 and pass the thread to P1, P1 to R3, R3 to R4, R4 to P2, P2 to P3, P3 to R5, R5 to R6, and so on until you reach P6. From P6 take the thread to R1, R1 to Q2, Q2 to Q3, Q3 to R2, R2 to R3, R3 to Q4 and so on until you reach R19. From R19 take the thread to Q18, Q18 to Q1, Q1 to Q17, Q17 to Q15 (which is also C1 and L5) and tie off. Tie on with a new colour at L6, L6 to Q1, Q1 to Q2, Q2 to L7, L7 to L8, L8 to Q3, Q3 to Q4, Q4 to L9 and so on until you reach L20. From L20 take the thread to L1 and tie off.

29

14 POND LIFE

You will need A piece of plywood or chipboard measuring 27in. (686mm.) by 15in. (381mm.) and at least ½in. (13mm.) thick; a piece of hessian 30in. (762mm.) by 18in. (457mm.); 1in. (25mm.) squared graph paper; 212 nails ½in. long; 136 nails ¾in. (19mm.) long and three balls of different coloured thread.

The design On 1in. squared graph paper make an actual size plan from the diagram using a dot to represent each nail. Mark all the lines as shown on the diagram and then fill in the right number of dots spacing them evenly along each line.

The board Make up the board as described in the introduction.

Positioning the nails Place the graph paper over the right side of the board, holding the corners in place with drawing pins. For the largest fish hammer in the longer nails about ½in. off the board, for the medium sized and smallest fish hammer in the shorter nails about ⅜in. (10mm.) and ¼in. (6mm.) off the board respectively. N.B. a circle round a junction of two lines indicates a nail which is common to two fish. Hammer the nail in at the higher of the two levels. Carefully remove the paper pattern.

Threading the design Tie the thread to A1 and pass to B13, B13 to B12, B12 to A2, A2 to A3, A3 to B11, B11 to B10, B10 to A4 and so on until you reach B3. From B3 pass the thread round B1, B1 to C1, C1 to C2, C2 to B2, B2 to B3, B3 to C3, C3 to C4 and so on until you reach C25 and tie off. Tie on again at D25 and pass the thread to A25, A25 to A24, A24 to D24, D24 to D23, D23 to A23 and so on until you reach A1. Take the thread to A5 and tie off. Tie on again at D7 and pass the thread to C31, C31 to C30, C30 to D8 D8 to D9, D9 to C29 and so on until you reach C7 and tie off. Thread the other two fish in the same manner using different coloured threads. When tying on fish two for the first time tie on at A1 and off at C23, for the second time on at D23 and off at A5 and for the third time on at D8 and off at C8. When tying on fish three for the first time tie on at A1 and off at C31, for the second time on at D32 and off at A5 and for the third time on at D14 and off at C14.

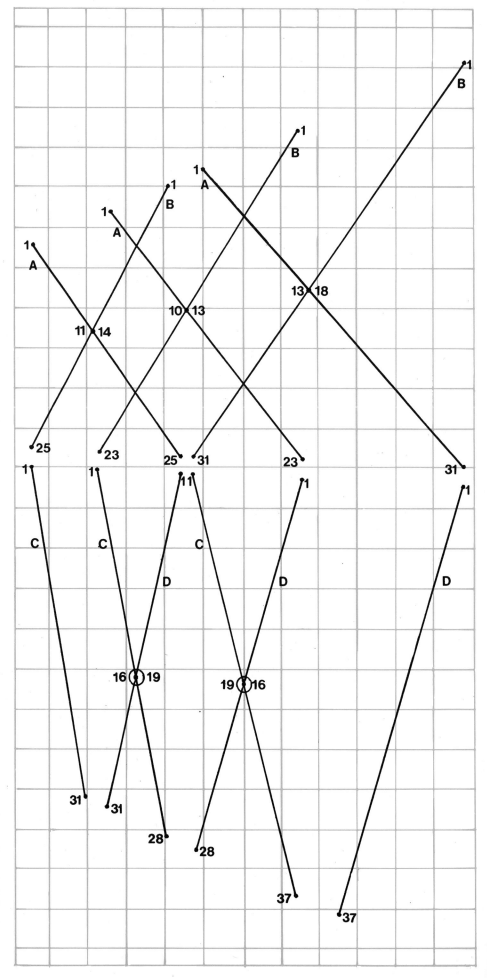

You will need A piece of plywood or chipboard measuring 19in. (483mm.) square and at least ½in. (13mm.) thick; a piece of felt large enough to cover the board plus 2in. (51mm.) all round; 1in. (25mm.) squared graph paper; 720 panel pins; clear household adhesive; and one ball of thread in red, one in turquoise blue and one in emerald green.

The design On 1in. squared graph paper make an actual size plan from the diagram, drawing three circles with 3¾in. (95mm.) radii with the circumferences touching as shown. From the centre point, draw a circle with 8in. (203mm.) radius to enclose the three smaller circles to form the 'tails'. Using a dot to represent each nail, space out the nails evenly in each row. Mark each line A1-A24, B1-B24 etc. as shown on the diagram.

The board Make up the board as described in the introduction.

Positioning the nails Place the graph paper over the right side of the board, holding the corners in place with drawing pins. Hammer the nails in position through the paper. Then carefully remove the paper.

Threading the design Tie the thread to any point marked A1 and pass to B1 in the same segment, (see diagram), B2 to A2, A2 to A3, A3 to B3, B3 to B4, B4 to A4 etc. Continue in this sequence tying off at B24. Thread the other eleven segments marked AB in the same way. Tie the thread to C1 in one circle and pass to D1 in the same segment, D1 to D2, D2 to C2, C2 to C3, C3 to D3, D3 to D4 etc. Thread the other two sections marked CD in the same way to complete the picture.

Place a spot of glue on each knot.

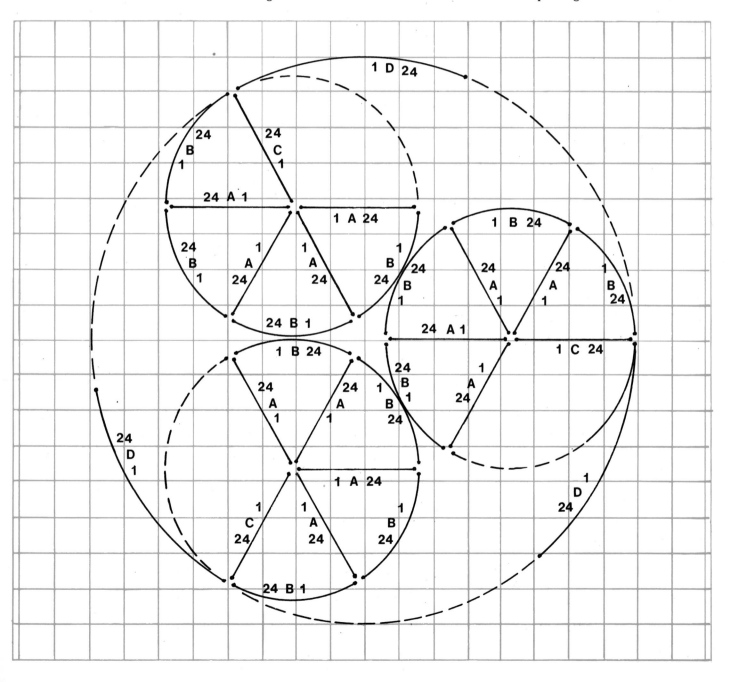

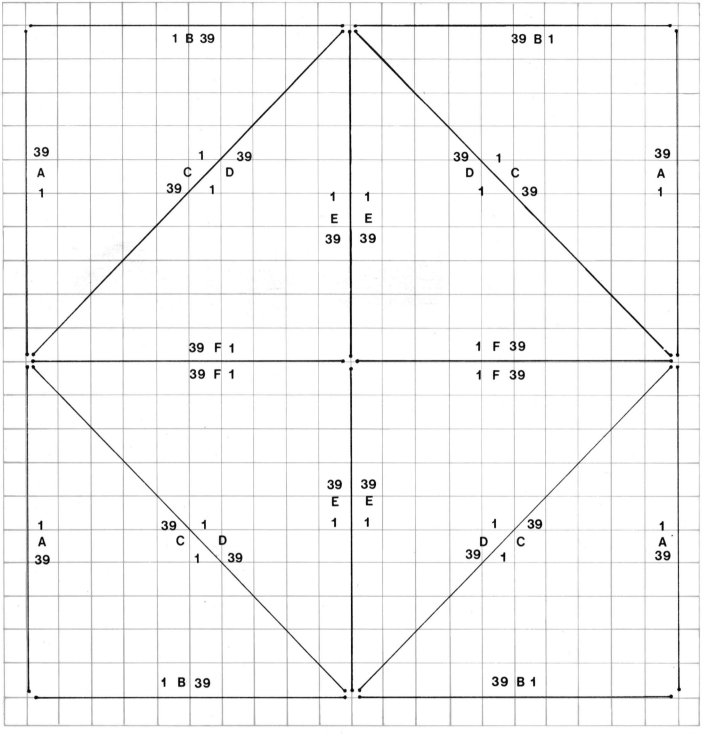

1 B 39   39 B 1

39   1 39   39 1   39
A   C   D   D   C   A
1   39 1   1   39   1

1   1
E   E
39 39

39 F 1   1 F 39
39 F 1   1 F 39

39 39
E   E
1   1

1   39 1   1   39   1
A   C   D   D   C   A
39   1 39   39 1   39

1 B 39   39 B 1

16
SUNBURST

You will need A piece of plywood or chipboard measuring 23in. (584mm.) square and at least ½in. (13mm.) thick; a piece of felt large enough to cover the board plus 2in. (51mm.) all round; 1in. (25mm.) squared graph paper; 624 panel pins; matt black paint; clear household adhesive and two balls of cotton thread.

The design On 1in. squared graph paper make an actual size plan from the diagram using a dot to represent each nail. It is important to space out the nails evenly in each row for a good result. Mark each line A1-A39, B1-B39 etc.

The board Make up the board as described in the introduction.

Positioning the nails Place the graph paper over the right side of the board, holding the corners in place with drawing pins. Hammer the nails in position through the paper. Then carefully remove the graph paper and paint the panel pins with matt black paint used sparingly. Allow to dry completely.

Threading the design This design is made up of eight triangles threaded separately. Tie the thread to any point A1 and pass the thread round B1 to C1, C1 to A2, A2 to B2 in the same triangle. Continue threading in this sequence tying off at C39. Thread the other three outer triangles in the same way. Then tie the thread to any point D1 and pass to E1 in the same triangle, E1 to F1, F1 to D2, D2 to E2, E2 to F2, F2 to D3 etc. Continue in this sequence tying off at F39. Thread the other three triangles in the same way.

Place a spot of glue on each knot to secure firmly in place.

9
MOON
BUGGY

PASSER BY

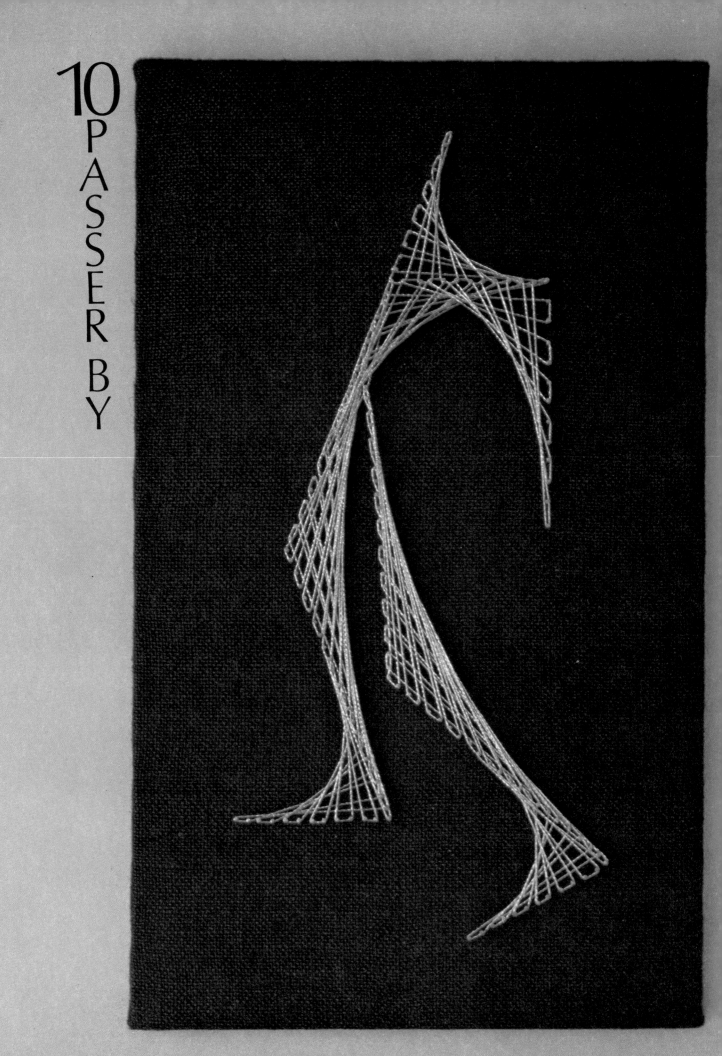

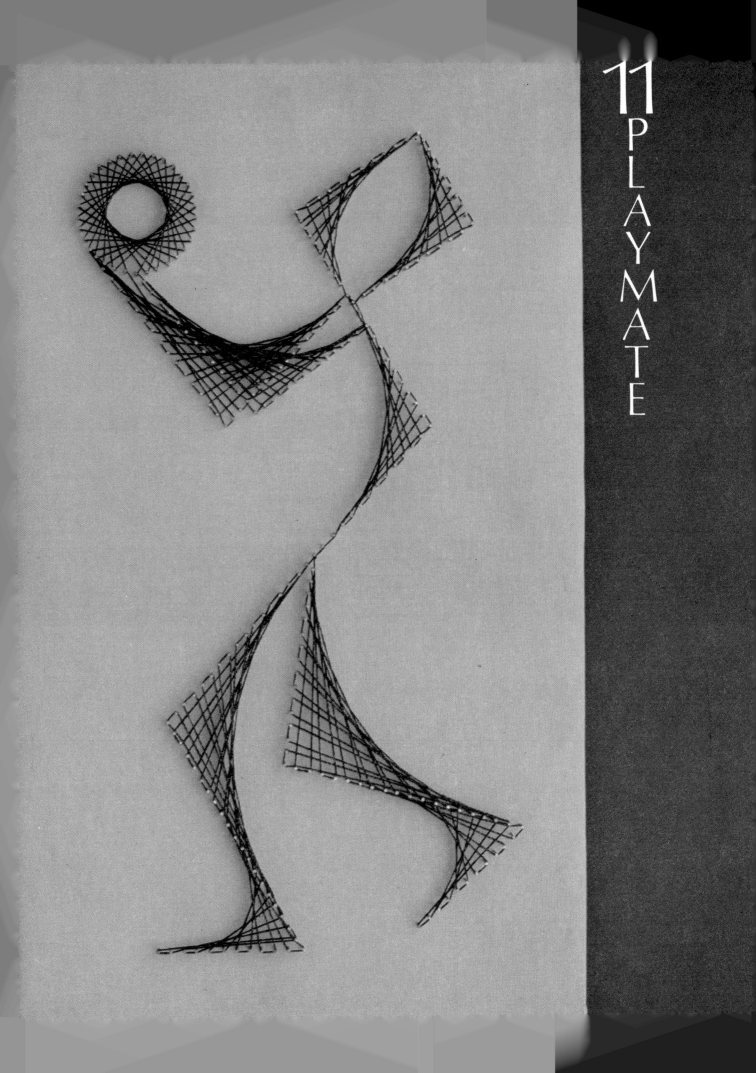

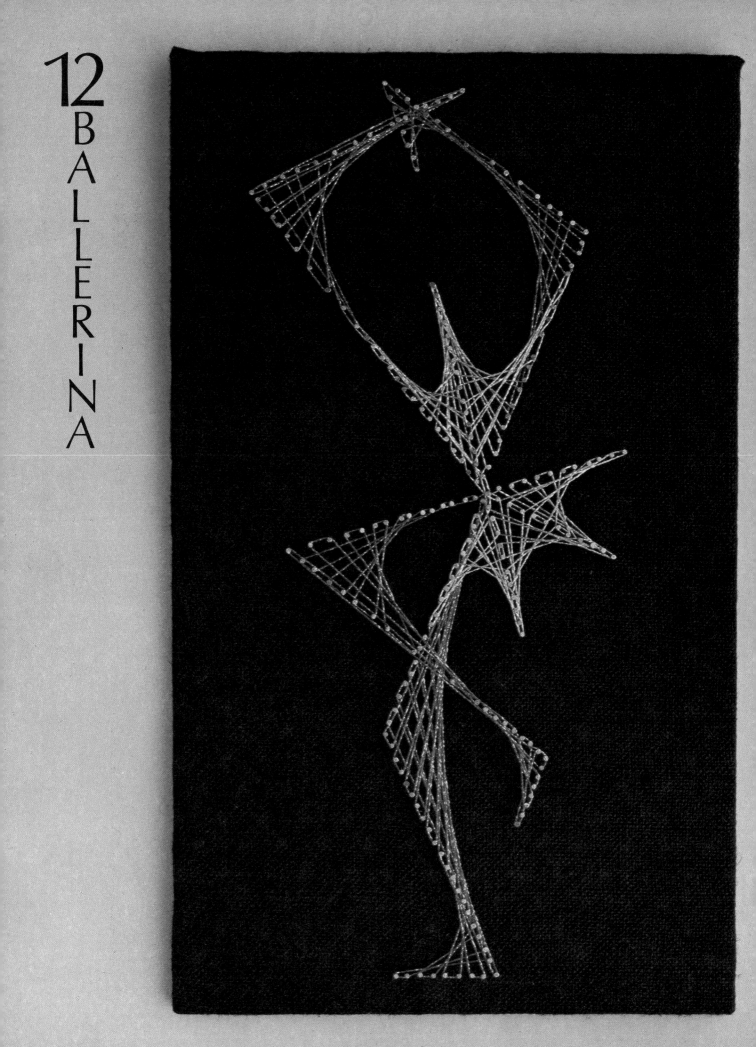

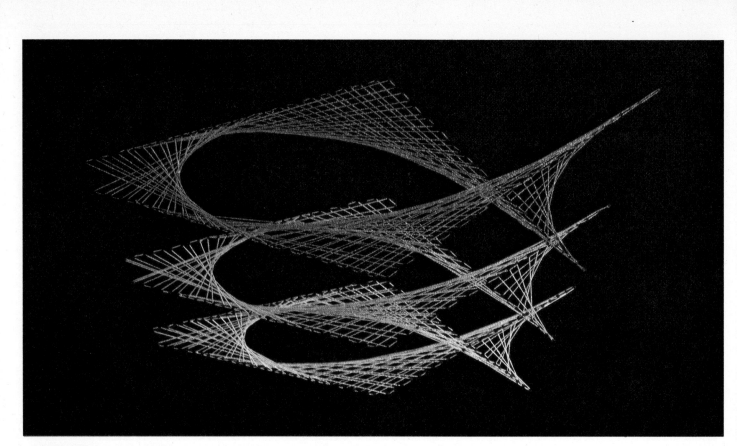

14
POND
LIFE

15
CATHERINE
WHEELS

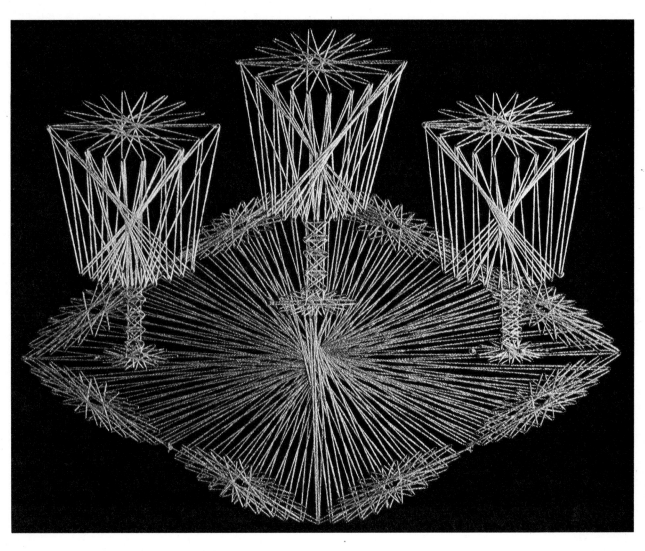

17
GOBLETS

16
SUNBURST

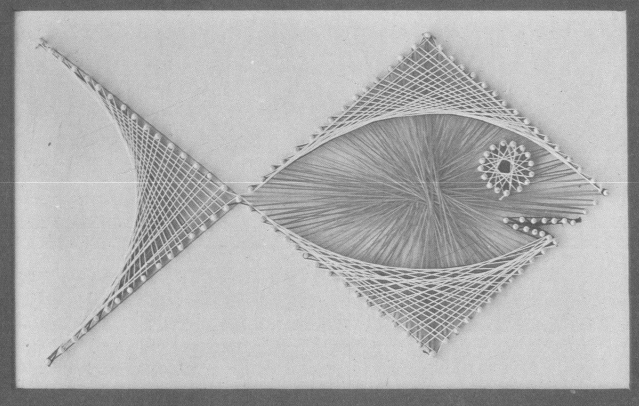

18
GOLDFISH

20
TRIBAL
MASK

21
BUTTERFLY

22
TALL
VASE

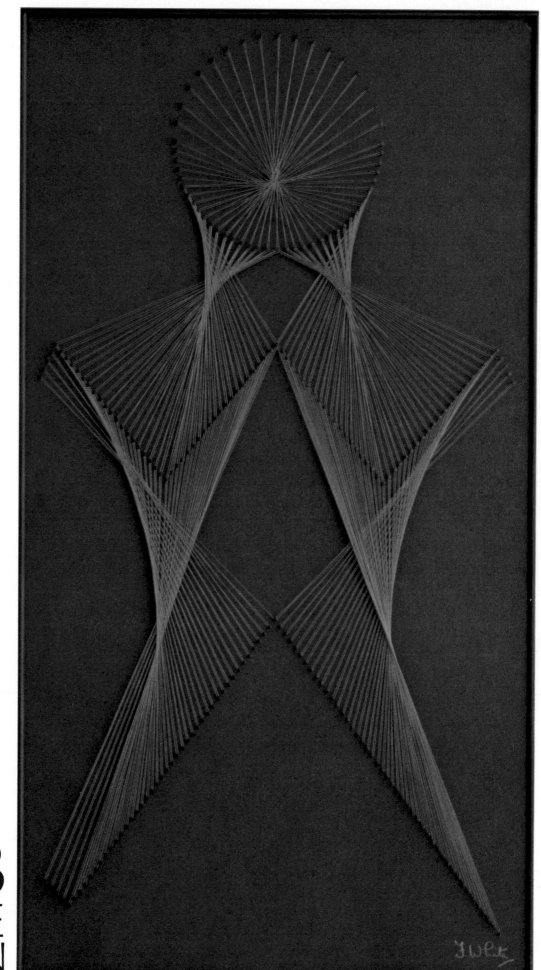

23
SPACE
MAN

24
SNOWFLAKE

17
GOBLETS

You will need A piece of plywood or chipboard measuring 16in. (406mm.) by 20in. (508mm.) and at least ½in. (13mm.) thick; a small tin of matt black paint; a paint brush; 1in. (25mm.) squared graph paper; 402 nails ½in. long; and some gold and silver thread.

The design On 1in. squared graph paper make an actual size plan from the diagram using a dot to represent each nail. The dots are equally spaced along the lines except where specifically marked.

The board Paint the board with black paint and leave until quite dry.

Positioning the nails Place the graph paper over the right side of the board, holding the corners in place with drawing pins. Hammer the nails in position through the paper, and remove the paper pattern carefully.

Threading the design Tie the gold thread to the nail marked A and pass to B, B to C, C to D, D to E and so on right round the outside of the tray. Now tie on at X1 and pass to X12, X12 to X23, X23 to X10, X10 to X21, X21 to X8 and so on until you return to X1. Now take the thread across to Y12 and repeat the previous sequence. Repeat the whole sequence starting at the other three points marked X. Tie on with silver at A1 and pass the thread to A9, A9 to A16, A16 to A8, A8 to A15 and so on until you return to A10. From A10 pass the thread to C9, C9 to C10, from C10 pass the thread up inside the line of nails to B7, across B6, round B5 and down inside the nails to C9, C9 to C8, C8 to C7, C7 to C6, C6 to C5, C5 to C4, C4 to C3, C3 to C2, C2 to C1, C1 to B7, B7 to B5, B5 to C2, C2 to C1, C1 to C4, C4 to C3, C3 to C6, C6 to C5, C5 to C8, C8 to C7, C7 to C10, C10 to C9. Repeat the threading for the stem taking care to pass the opposite way round each nail. Tie on again at D1 and pass the thread to D9, D9 to D18, D18 to D8, and so on until you reach D10. From D10 pass the thread back to D1, D1 to B1, B1 to D18, D18 to B2, B2 to D17, D17 to B3, B3 to D16, D16 to B4, B4 to D15, D15 to B5, B5 to D14, D14 to B7, B7 to D13 and so on until you reach D10. From D10 pass the thread to B1, B1 to D11, D11 to B2, B2 to D12 and so on missing out B6. Tie off at B11. Repeat for the other two glasses.

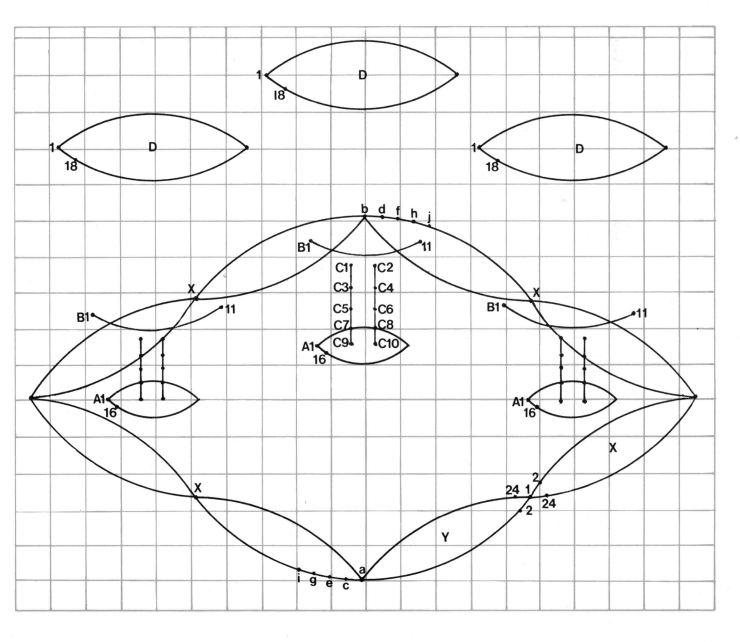

18 GOLDFISH

You will need A piece of plywood or chipboard measuring 24in. (610mm.) by 14in. (356mm.) and at least ½in. (13mm.) thick; a small tin of white paint; a paint brush; 1in. (25mm.) squared graph paper; 222 nails ½in. long and some red, orange and white thread.

The design On 1in. squared graph paper make an actual size plan using a dot to represent each nail. The dots should be regularly spaced along all lines.

The board Make up the board as described in the introduction.

Positioning the nails Place the graph paper over the right side of the board, holding the corners in place with drawing pins. Hammer the nails in position through the paper, and remove the paper pattern carefully.

Threading the design Tie on with orange at A1 and pass the thread to A65, A65 to A2, A2 to A66 and so on using B12 between A87 and A88, tie off when you return to A1. Tie on with red at A87 and pass the thread to B12, B12 to A88, A88 to B11, B11 to B23, B23 to B10, B10 to B22, B22 to B9 and so on tying off at A87. Tie on again with red at A94 and pass to A1, A1 to A95, A95 to A2, A2 to A96 and

so on until you reach A33. From A33 take the thread to A65, A65 to A34, A34 to A66 and so on until you reach A87 and tie off. Repeat with white cotton. Tie on at C1 with red and pass to C17, C17 to C2, C2 to C18 and so on tying off at C1. Tie on again with white at C17, C17 to C32, C32 to C15, C15 to C30, C30 to C13 and so on tying off at C17. Tie on again with orange at D1 and pass to D33, D33 to D2, D2 to D34 and so on tying off at D65. Tie on again with red at D65 and pass to D33, D33 to D64, D64 to D32 and so on tying off at D1. Tie on again with white at D1 and repeat as for orange.

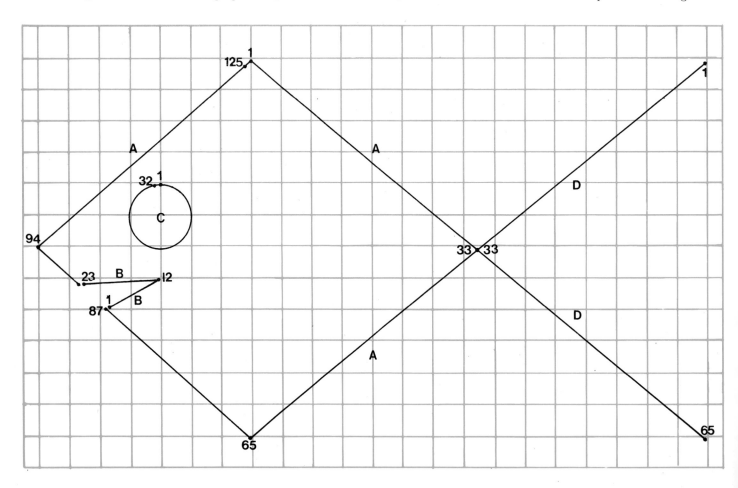

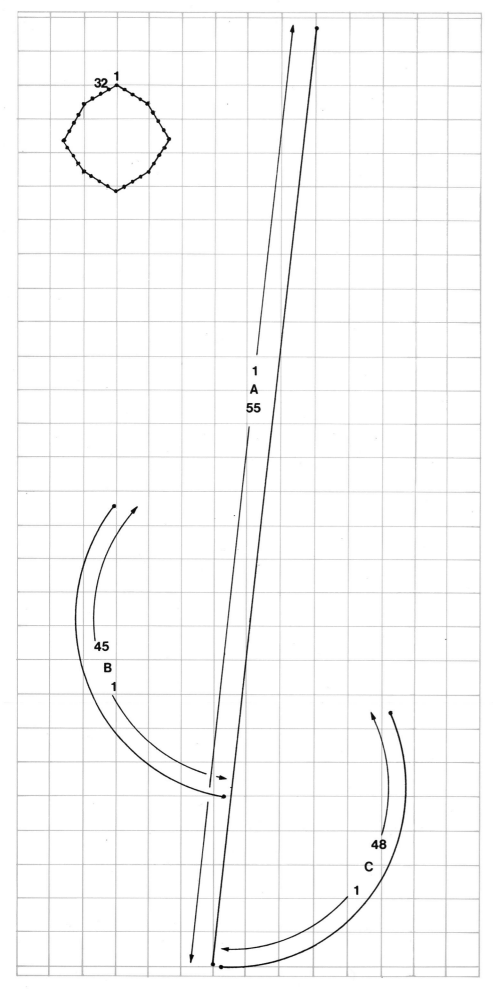

19 POLAR PEAK

You will need A piece of plywood or chipboard measuring 30in. (762mm.) by 12in. (305mm.) and at least ½in. (13 mm.) thick; a piece of contoured cork the same size (painted with emulsion to achieve the required colour); 1in. (25 mm.) squared graph paper; 180 panel pins; a ball of thread in ice blue and some clear household adhesive.

The design On 1in. squared graph paper make an actual size plan from the diagram, using a dot to represent each nail. It is important to space out the nails evenly in each row for a good result. Mark each line A1-55, B1-45, C1-48 etc. as shown on the diagram.

The board Using clear household adhesive stick the contoured cork to the plywood backing.

Positioning the nails Place the graph paper over the right side of the board, holding the corners in place with drawing pins. Hammer the nails in position through the paper. Then remove the graph paper.

Threading the design Tie the thread to A1 and pass to B1, B1 to B2 (see diagram) B2 to A2, A2 to A3, A3 to B3 etc. Continue in this sequence to B7, pass to B8, B8 to A8, A8 to C1, C1 to C2, C2 to A9, A9 to B9, B9 to B10, B10 to A10, A10 to C3, C3 to C4, C4 to A11, A11 to B11, B11 to B12, B12 to A12 etc. Continue in this sequence to B45 and tie off. Tie on again at A46 and take the thread to C39, C39 to C40, C40 to A47, A47 to A48, A48 to C41, C41 to C42, C42 to A49 etc. tying off at A55.

The circle is not threaded continuously. Tie the thread to pin 1 and pass round pin 9 to pin 17 to pin 25 and back to pin 1 and tie off. Tie the thread to pin 2 pass round pin 10 to pin 18 to pin 26 and back to pin 2 and tie off. Continue threading the squares in this way to complete the centre circle.

Place a spot of glue on each knot to make it more secure.

20 TRIBAL MASK

You will need A piece of plywood or chipboard measuring 31in. (787mm.) by 15in. (381mm.) and at least ½in. (13mm.) thick; a small tin of matt black paint; a paint brush; 1in. (25mm.) squared graph paper; 407 nails ¾in. (19mm.) long and a ball of blue thread.

The design On 1in. squared graph paper make an actual size plan from the diagram using a dot to represent each nail. Mark each line A1-43, B1-43 etc. spacing the dots evenly along the line.

The board Paint the board with matt black paint and leave until quite dry.

Positioning the nails Place the graph paper over the right side of the board, holding the corners in place with drawing pins. Hammer the nails in position through the paper and then remove the paper carefully.

Threading the design Tie the thread to A43 and pass to A1 *inside* the line A, A1 to B1, B1 to A2, A2 to B2, B2 to A3 and so on until you reach B42 (which is also C1). From C1 pass the thread to D1, D1 to C2, C2 to D2, until you reach C13. From C13 pass the thread to A11, A11 to C12, C12 to A10 and so on until you reach D1 (which is also E1). From E1 pass the thread to E24, E24 to E2, E2 to E25 and so on until you reach E65. From E65 pass the thread to E6, E6 to E66, E66 to E7 until you reach E1 (which is also F1). From F1 pass the thread to F46, F46 to F2, F2 to F47 and so on until you reach F91 (which also C13 and E47). To thread the eyes tie on at G1 and pass over the top of the inner ring of nails to G23. No thread should encircle any of the nails of the inner ring. From G23 to G2, G2 to G24, G24 to G3 and so on until you reach G1 and tie off. Repeat this sequence for eye H.

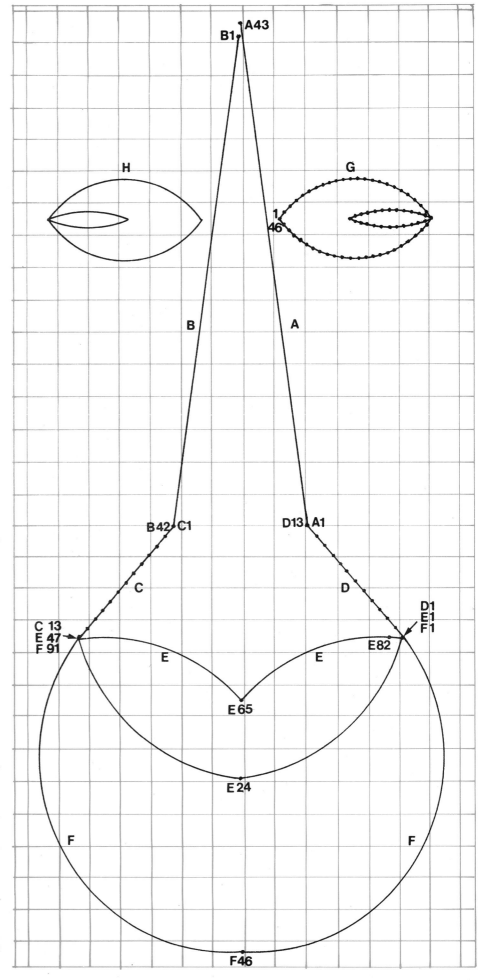

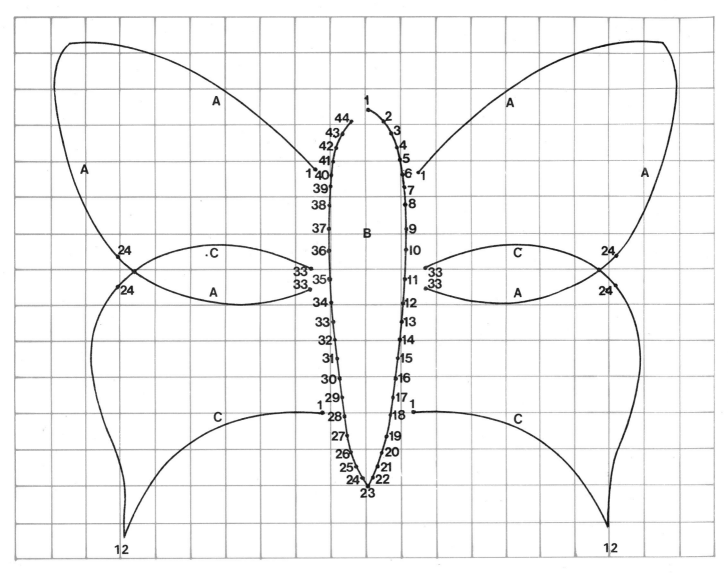

21 BUTTERFLY

You will need A piece of plywood or chipboard measuring 20in. (508mm.) by 16in. (406mm.) and at least ½in. (13mm.) thick; a small tin of matt white paint; a paint brush; 174 nails ½in. long; 1in. (25mm.) squared graph paper and some gold, silver, blue and white thread.

The design On 1in. squared graph paper make an actual size plan from the diagram using a dot to represent each nail. The dots should be regularly spaced along each line except for line B

where you should follow the diagram exactly.

The board Make up the board as described in the introduction.

Positioning the nails Place the graph paper over the right side of the board, holding the corners in place with drawing pins. Hammer the nails in position through the paper, and remove the paper pattern carefully.

Threading the design Tie on with silver at B11 and pass to A15, A15 to B10, B10 to A16, A16 to B9, B9 to A17, A17 to B8, B8 to A18, A18 to B7, B7 to A19, A19 to A1, and so on until you reach A33. From A33 pass the thread to C15, C15 to B11, B11 to C14, C14 to C33, C33 to C13, C13 to C32, C32 to C2, C2 to C31 and so on right round the wing until you return to B11 and tie off. Tie on again with blue at B7 and pass to A14, A14 to B8, B8 to A13 and so on until you reach A17. From A17 take the thread to A33, A33 to A18 and so on tying off at A28. Tie on again in blue at B12 and pass the thread to C20, C20 to B13, B13 to C21 and so on until you reach C25. From C25 pass the thread to

C1 and continue round tying off when you return to B12. Tie on again with white at C25 (which is also A25) and pass the thread to B11, B11 to C26, C26 to A33, A33 to C27 and so on until you return to C25 and tie off. Tie on again with gold at B18 and pass to C12, C12 to C1, C1 to C13, C13 to C2 and so on until you reach C30. From C30 take the thread to A28, A28 to A14, A14 to A27, A27 to A13, A13 to A26 and so on until you reach B7 and tie off. Repeat for the other side of the butterfly. Tie on again in gold at B1 and pass to B36, B36 to B2, B2 to B37 and so on until you return to B1 and tie off. Tie on again at B23 and pass to B34, B34 to B22, B22 to B33, B33 to B21 and so on until you return to B23 and tie off. Tie on again at B6 and pass to B39, B39 to B8, B8 to B37, B37 to B10, B10 to right wing A33, A33 to left wing C33, C33 to B34, B34 to B13, B13 to B32, B32 to B15, B15 to B30, B30 to B17, B17 to B28, B28 to B18 and return in reverse order tying off at B40. Tie on again in silver at B40 and pass the thread to B17, B17 to B39, B39 to B16 and so on until you reach B6 and tie off.

22 TALL VASE

You will need A piece of plywood or chipboard measuring 27in. (686mm.) by 10in. (254mm.) and at least ½in. (13 mm.) thick; a piece of hessian 30in. (762mm.) by 13in. (330mm.); 1in. (25 mm.) squared graph paper; 139 nails ½in. long; about two dozen tacks and two balls of different coloured thread.

The design On 1in. squared graph paper make an actual size plan from the diagram using a dot to represent each nail. Mark each line A1-27, B1-17 etc. spacing the dots evenly except where the exact spacing is marked.

The board Make up the board as described in the introduction.

Positioning the nails Place the graph paper over the right side of the board, holding the corners in place with drawing pins. Hammer the nails in position through the paper. Then carefully remove the graph paper.

Threading the design Tie the thread to A1 and pass to B1, B1 to A11, A11 to A12, A12 to B2, B2 to B3, B3 to A13, A13 to B14, B14 to B15, B15 to C13, C13 to B4, B4 to A14, A14 to C14, C14 to B14, B14 to B13, B13 to A8, A8 to C5, C5 to C4, C4 to B8, B8 to A2, A2 to C10, C10 to C11, C11 to B17, B17 to C1, C1 to C2, C2 to A10, A10 to A9, A9 to C3, C3 to B9, B9 to A3, A3 to C9, C9 to C8, C8 to A5, A5 to A4, A4 to B10, B10 to C2, C2 to B10, B10 to B11, B11 to A6, A6 to C7, C7 to B6, B6 to B7, B7 to C6, C6 to A7, A7 to B12, B12 to B16, B16 to C12, C12 to C8, C8 to B5 and tie off. Tie on again with a different colour at D1 and pass the thread to C27, C27 to C26, C26 to D2, D2 to D3, D3 to C25, C25 to C24 and so on until you reach C2. From C2 pass the thread round C1 to B1, B1 to B3, B3 to B2, B2 to B5, B5 to B4, B4 to B7, B7 to B6 and so on until you reach B17. From B17 pass the thread to F25, F25 to F24, F24 to A2, A2 to A3, A3 to F23, F23 to F22, F22 to A4, A4 to A5 and so on until you reach F1 and tie off. Tie on again with the original colour at D19, D19 to G1, G1 to F1, F1 to D18, D18 to D17, D17 to F2, F2 to F3 and so on until you reach F19 and tie off. Tie on again with the same colour at D10, D10 to G1, G1 to G2, G2 to D9, D9 to D8, D8 to G3 and so on until you reach D1. From D1 pass the thread round E1 and up to F9, F9 to F8, F8 to E2, E2 to E3 and so on until you reach G1 and tie off.

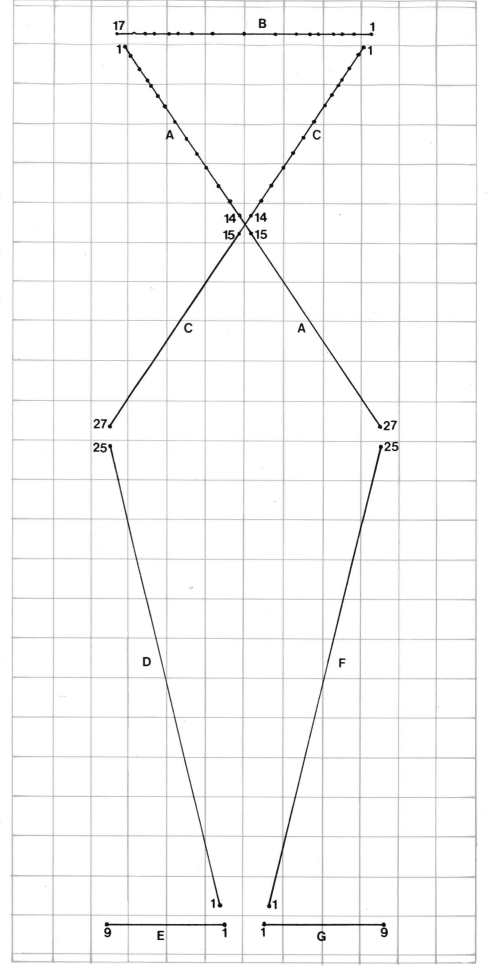

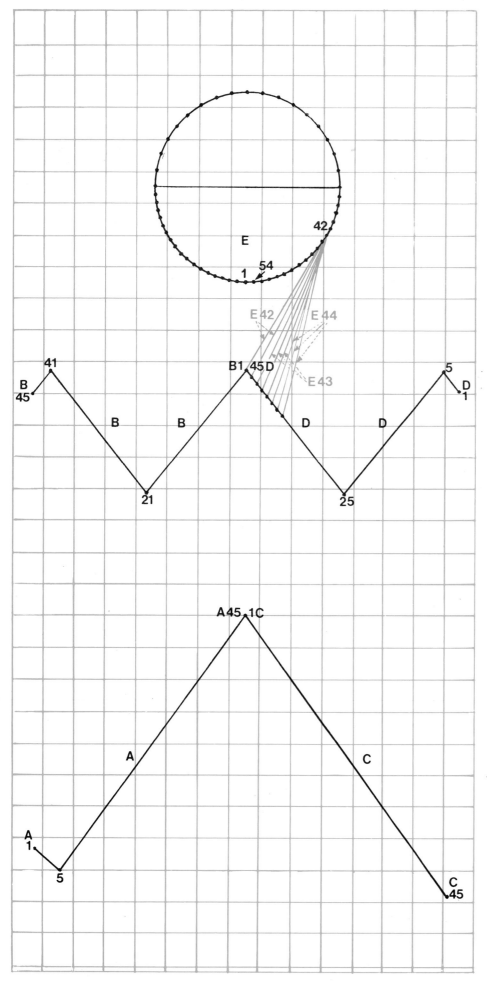

23
SPACE MAN

You will need A piece of plywood or chipboard measuring 27in. (686mm.) by 15in. (381mm.) and at least ½in. (13 mm.) thick; a small tin of matt black paint; a paint brush; 1in. (25mm.) squared graph paper; 232 nails ¾in. (19mm.) long and a ball of green thread.

The design On 1in. squared graph paper make an actual size plan from the diagram using a dot to represent each nail. Mark each line A1-45, B1-45, C1-45 and D1-D45 spacing the dots evenly and draw the circle E 6in. (152mm.) in diameter. The space between the dots on the upper half of the circle should be exactly twice the space between those on the lower half. The measurements are approximately ½in. and ¼in. but it is advisable to use a protractor in which case the dots are 10° apart on the upper circle and 5° apart on the lower one.

The board Paint the board with matt black paint and leave until quite dry.

Positioning the nails. Place the graph paper over the right side of the board, holding the corners in place with drawing pins. Hammer the nails in position through the paper and then remove the paper carefully.

Threading the design Tie the thread to A1 and pass to B1, B1 to A2, A2 to B2 and continue this sequence until you reach A45 (which is also C1). From C1 pass the thread to D1, D1 to C2, C2 to D2 until you reach D45. Threading the circle is quite complex. From D45 pass the thread to E42, E42 to D44, D44 to E42, E42 to D43, D43 to E43, E43 to D42, D42 to E43, E43 to D41, D41 to E43, and continue in this sequence until you reach E1 from D5. In this way the thread passes from one nail on circle E to three nails on line D. (Except for the thread from E42 which passes to only two nails on line D.) From E1 pass the thread to B41, B41 to E1, E1 to B40, B40 to E1, E1 to B39, B39 to E2 and continue in this sequence from one nail on circle E to three on line B until you reach E14. From E14 pass the thread to E40, E40 to E15, E15 to E41 and continue in this sequence — tying off at E14.

55

24 SNOWFLAKE

You will need A piece of plywood or chipboard measuring 22in. (559mm.) square and at least $\frac{1}{2}$in. (13mm.) thick; a small tin of matt black paint; a paint brush; 1in. (25mm.) squared graph paper; 220 nails $\frac{1}{2}$in. long and three balls of different coloured thread — we used green, white and mauve.

The design On 1in. squared graph paper make an actual size plan from the diagram using a dot to represent each nail. The dots on all lines should be regularly spaced.

The board Make up the board as described in the introduction.

Positioning the nails Place the graph paper over the right side of the board, holding the corners in place with drawing pins. Hammer the nails in position through the paper, and remove the paper pattern carefully.

Threading the design Tie on with green thread at A1 and working the thread clockwise round the nail, pass it to A7, A7 to A1, A1 to A8, A8 to A1 and so on until you reach A21. From A21 pass the thread to A1 and working anti-

clockwise round the nail pass it to A14, A14 to A2, A2 to A15, A15 to A3 and so on until you return to A1 and tie off. Repeat for B, C, D, E and F. C and F have fewer nails but the procedure is identical. Tie on again with white at G1 and pass the thread clockwise round the nail to G2, G2 to G1, G1 to G3, G3 to G1, G1 to G4, and so on until you return to G1 from G26. Now pass the thread to G14, G14 to G2, G2 to G15, G15 to G3 and so on tying off when you return to G1. Repeat for H, I, J, K, and L. Tie on again with mauve at M37 and pass the thread clockwise round the nail to M4, M4 to M37, M37 to M5, M5 to M37 and so on until you return to M4. From M4 pass the thread to M28, M28 to M3, M3 to M27, M27 to M2, M2 to M26 and so on until you return to M4 and tie off.

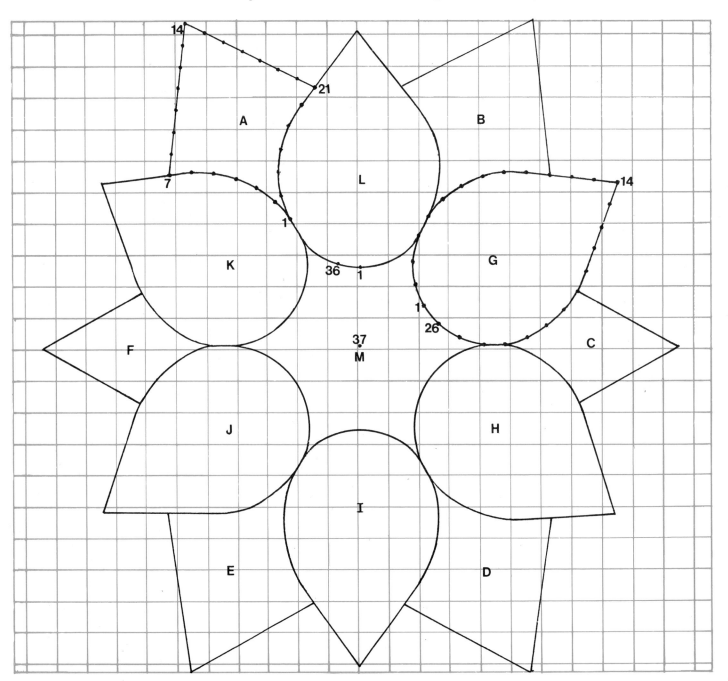

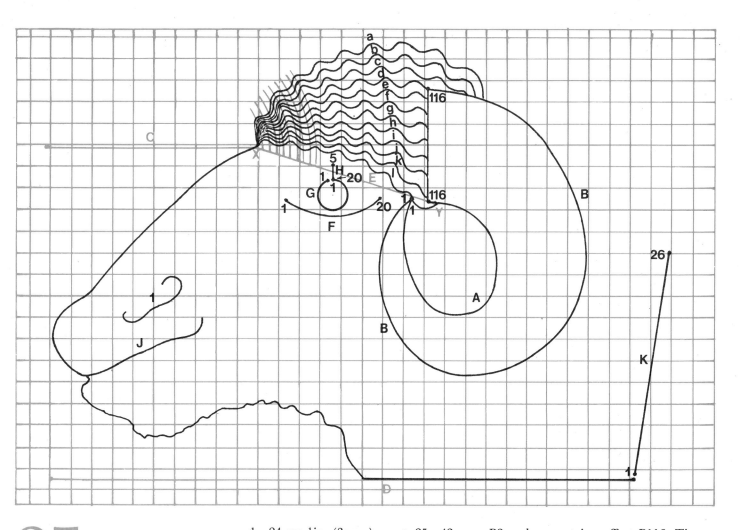

25 ARIES

You will need A piece of plywood or chipboard measuring 32in. (813mm.) by 22in. (559mm.) and at least ½in. (13mm.) thick; a piece of felt large enough to cover the board plus 2in. (51mm.) all round; 1in. (25mm.) squared graph paper; about 975 nails ½in. long; clear household adhesive; several balls of different coloured thread.

The design On 1in. squared graph paper make an actual size plan from the diagram using a dot to represent each nail. The spacing of the dots in this design is very complicated. Mark in those on lines A and B first; on line A they are evenly spaced but on line B

1—24 are ⅛in. (3mm.) apart, 25—42 are $\frac{3}{16}$in. (5mm.) apart and 43—116 are ¼in. (6mm.) apart. Now draw in lines C, D and E which are not part of the design. Mark off points at $\frac{3}{16}$in. intervals along these lines and join the dots along D with those on C and E. This will give you the position of the dots which make up the face outline and also those which make up the mouth and nostril. For the fleece place the point of a compass at X and, using the dots already marked along E swing the compass round to give you all the dots on the fleece. Fill in those at the end by hand. The dots on lines F, G, H and K are evenly spaced.

The board Make up the board as described in the introduction.

Positioning the nails Place the graph paper over the right side of the board, holding the corners in place with drawing pins. Hammer the nails in position through the paper, and remove the paper pattern carefully.

Threading the design Tie the thread to A1 and pass it to B1, B1 to A2, A2 to

B2 and so on tying off at B116. Tie on again at the tip of the nose and work straight up and down right across the head. When you come to the end of the nails which make the bottom line of the fleece, thread from line D up to the bottom edge of the horn and continue up the left side of the horn from line K. If in doubt consult the photograph. Tie off at K26. Tie on again at X and pass it to the first nail on line A, from here pass it to line B linking up all the nails on these two lines. Now return the thread the same way to X. Proceed in the same manner linking up the other pairs of lines. Tie on again at G1 and pass to G8, G8 to G2, G2 to G9, G9 to G3, G3 to G10 and so on until you return to G1 and tie off. Tie on again at F1 and pass to G1, G1 to F2, F2 to G2 and so on tying off at F20. Tie on again at F1 and pass the thread over H5 to F20, F20 to H4 to F1, F1 to H3 to F20, F20 to H2 to F1, F1 to H1 to F20 and tie off. To pick out lines I and J thread along and back in dark thread.

26 TAURUS

You will need A piece of plywood or chipboard measuring 32in. (813mm.) by 22in. (559mm.) and at least ½in. (13mm.) thick; a piece of felt large enough to cover the board plus 2in. (51mm.) all round; 1in. (25mm.) squared graph paper; 798 nails ½in. long; clear household adhesive and some gold, silver, red white and brown thread.

The design On 1in. squared graph paper make an actual size plan from the diagram using a dot to represent each nail. The dots should be regularly spaced along each line.

The board Make up the board as described in the introduction.

Positioning the nails Place the graph paper over the right side of the board, holding the corners in place with drawing pins. Hammer the nails in position through the paper, and remove the paper pattern carefully.

Threading the design Tie the gold thread to C and pass it to A1, A1 to B1, B1 to A2 and so on until you reach B65. From B65, B66, B67 and B68 take the thread to A64 and tie off. Repeat for the other horn noting that C is replaced by E2. Tie on again with red at L1 and pass to K1, K1 to L3, L3 to K2 and so on, threading alternate nails on line L; until you reach L19 and tie off at L19. Tie on again with white at O1 and pass the thread to L10, L10 to L20, L20 to O1, O1 to L11, L11 to O2, O2 to L12 and so on until you reach L20. From L20 pass the thread to O1 and tie off. Tie on again with red at L1 and pass the thread to O1, O1 to L2, L2 to O2 and so on until you reach L10 and tie off. Tie on again with red at M1 and pass the thread to

N15, N15 to N1, N1 to M1, M1 to N2, N2 to M2, M2 to N3 and so on tying off at N15. Tie on again with red at P1 and pass the thread from P1 to R1, R1 to P2, P2 to R2 and so on until you reach P9. From P9 take the thread to Q9, Q9 to P8, P8 to Q8 and so on tying off at P1. Tie on with brown at U31 and pass to W1, W1 to U31, U31 to W2 and so on tying off when you reach U31 from W11. Tie on with red at T1 and pass to U1, U1 to T2, T2 to U2 etc. tying off at U31. Tie on again with silver at V1, V1 to W1, W1 to V2, V2 to W2 and so on tying off at W6. Tie on again with brown at Z1, Z1 to Y2, Y2 to Z2, Z2 to Y3 and so on tying off at Z6. Tie on again with red at S1 and pass to S17, S17 to S2, S2 to S16 and so on tying off at S1. Tie on again with white at Y1 and pass to X1, X1 to Y2, Y2 to X2 and so on tying off at X11. Tie on again with silver thread at D1 and pass it to D6, D6 to E6, E6 to D1, D1 to E2, E2 to D2, D2 to E3 and so on tying off at E6. Thread F, G and H, J in the same way. Now fill in the other side of the bull in exactly the same way.

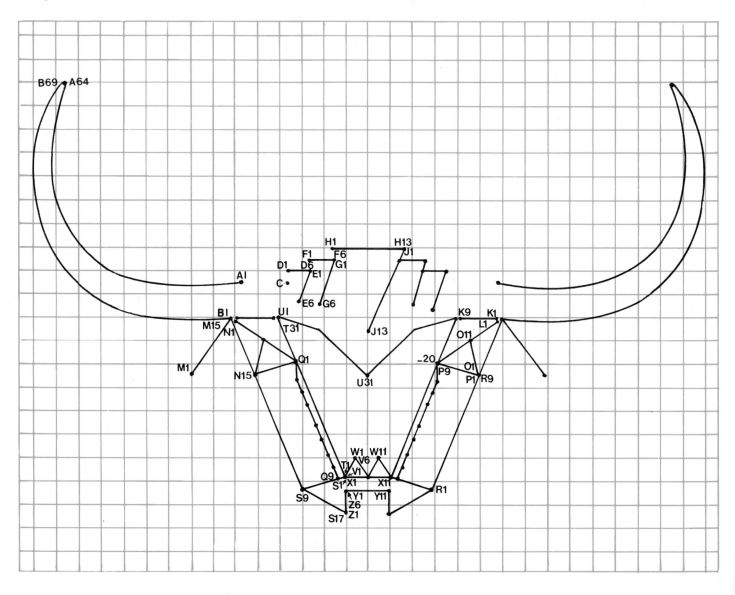

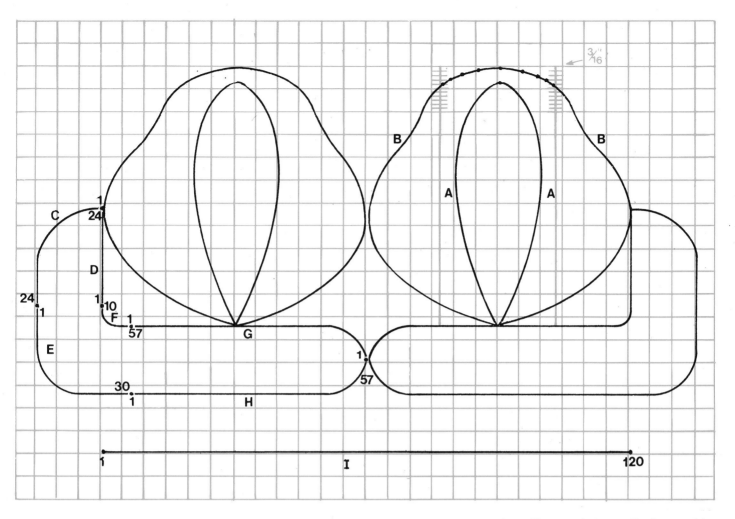

GEMINI

You will need A piece of plywood or chipboard measuring 32in. (813mm.) by 22in. (559mm.) and at least ½in. (13mm.) thick; a piece of felt large enough to cover the board plus 2in. (51mm.) all round; 800 nails ½in. long; 1in. (25mm.)

squared graph paper; clear household adhesive and three different coloured reels of thread — we used silver, yellow and red.

The design On 1in. squared graph paper make an actual size plan from the diagram, using a dot to represent each nail. Draw in lines A and B and the parallel lines as shown on the diagram. On the parallel lines (which are *not* part of the design) mark off $\frac{3}{16}$in. (5mm.) intervals and with a ruler mark off the dots on lines A and B. On all other lines the dots are equally spaced.

The board Make up the board as described in the introduction.

Positioning the nails Place the graph paper over the right side of the board, holding the corners in place with drawing

pins. Hammer the nails in position through the paper, and remove the paper pattern carefully.

Threading the design Tie the thread to A1 and pass across to the parallel point on line B, back to A2 and so on right round tying off at the end of line A. Repeat for the other side. Tie on again at G1 and pass to H57, H57 to G2, G2 to H56 and so on until you reach F1. From F1 take the thread round three nails on line E and back to E2. From E2 take the thread round the next three nails on line E and so on until you reach C24. Complete the section by threading as between line G and H. Repeat for the other side. Tie on again at I1 and pass the thread up to the parallel point on line H. Thread the whole line tying off at I120.

28 CANCER

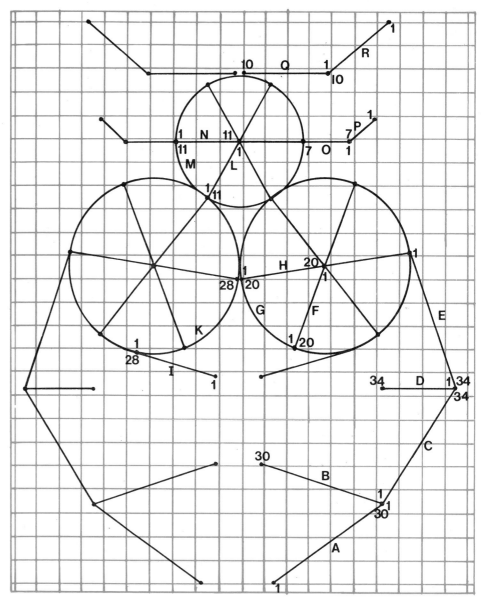

You will need A piece of plywood or chipboard measuring 32in. (813mm.) by 22in. (559mm.) at least ½in. (13mm.) thick; a piece of felt large enough to cover the board plus 2in. (51mm.) all round; 1in. (25mm.) squared graph paper; about 960 nails ½in. long; clear household adhesive and several different coloured reels of thread.

The design On 1in. squared graph paper make an actual size plan from the diagram using a dot to represent each nail. Mark in lines A1-A30, B1-B30 etc. spacing the dots regularly along each line.

The board Make up the board as described in the introduction.

Positioning the nails Place the graph paper over the right side of the board, holding the corners in place with drawing pins. Hammer the nails in position through the paper, and remove the paper pattern carefully.

Threading the design Tie the thread to A1 and pass it to B1, B1 to A2, A2 to B2 and so on until you reach B30 and tie off. Repeat for the other side. Tie on again at C1 and pass the thread to D1, D1 to C2, C2 to D2, D2 to C3 and so on until you reach D34. From D34 pass the thread to E34, E34 to D33, D33 to E33 and so on until you reach E1 and tie off. Repeat for the other side. Tie on again at G1

(which is also F20) and pass to H1 (which is also G20), H1 to F1 (which is also H20), F1 to G2, G2 to H2, H2 to F2, F2 to G3 and so on until the segment is completed. Repeat for all identical segments and use the same sequence for L, M, N. Tie on again at I1 and pass to K1, K1 to I2, I2 to K2 and so on tying off at K28. Repeat for the other side. Tie on again at P1 and pass to O1, O1 to P2, P2 to O2 and so on tying off at O7. Repeat for the other side and use the same sequence for the lines R, Q.

29 LEO

Positioning the nails Place the graph paper over the right side of the board, holding the corners in place with drawing pins. Hammer the nails in position through the paper, and remove the paper pattern carefully.

You will need A piece of plywood or chipboard measuring 32in. (813mm.) by 22in. (559mm.) and at least ½in. (13mm.) thick; a piece of felt large enough to cover the board plus 2in. (51mm.) all round; 1in. (25mm.) squared graph paper; 1070 nails ½in. long; clear household adhesive; gold, black and silver thread.

The design On 1in. squared graph paper make an actual size plan from the diagram using a dot to represent each nail. Our version has 600 nails along line A and 300 along line B. They are evenly spaced except for A250-A350 which are twice as far apart as the rest of the nails. If you wish to simplify the pattern you can cut down the number of nails providing you still have twice as many along line A as along line B. All other nails are equally spaced along their lines.

The board Make up the board as described in the introduction.

Threading the design Tie the gold thread to A1 and pass it to B1, B1 to A2, A2 to B1, B1 to A3, A3 to B2, B2 to A4, A4 to B2 and so on until you reach A600 and tie off. In this way for every nail used on line B, two are used on line A. Tie on again with white at C10 and pass the thread to H35, H35 to C10, C10 to H34, H34 to C10 and so on until you reach H25. From H25 take the thread back to C10 and then, passing under the eye, across to the nail on line B which is level with line C. From the same point line B (let us call it X) pass the thread to H15, H15 to X, X to H14, H14 to X, X to H13 and so on until you reach H5. From H5 take the thread to X and over the top of the eye to C10 and tie off. Work the other eye in the same way. Tie on again at C1 and pass to D1, D1 to C1, C1 to D2, D2 to C1, C1 to D3, D3 to C2, C2 to D4, D4 to C2, C2 to D5, D5 to C2, C2 to D6, D6 to C3 and so on until you reach D30 and tie off at C10. Tie on again at F1 and pass to G1, G1 to F2, F2 to G2, G2 to F3 and so on until you reach G20. Take the thread to F1, back to G20 and tie off.

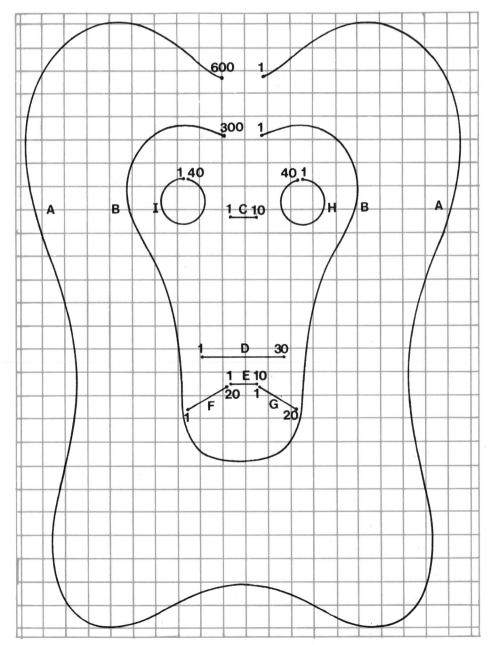

30 VIRGO

You will need A piece of plywood or chipboard measuring 32in. (813mm.) by 22in. (559mm.) and at least ½in. (13mm.) thick; a piece of felt large enough to cover the board plus 2in. (51mm.) all round; 1in. (25mm.) squared graph paper with ¼in. (6mm.) subdivisions; about 1360 nails ½in. long; clear household adhesive and four different coloured reels of thread — we used turquoise, light blue, dark blue and silver.

The design On 1in. squared graph paper make an actual size plan from the diagram, using a dot to represent each nail. This design has a considerable number of nails, if you wish you can halve the number in each line. Draw in all the lines as shown on the diagram and mark 64 dots along line B at regular intervals. Put a ruler at X and align it with B1 where the ruler crosses lines A and C mark dots A1 and C1. Mark dots A2-A64 and C2-C64 in the same way and then fill in dots at ¼in. intervals from A2 to C2, A4 to C4, A6 to C6 and so on until you reach 64. Mark 70 dots along line D at regular intervals and 35 dots along lines E, F, G and H also at regular intervals. Mark in the features of the face, exactly as shown on the diagram.

The board Make up the board as described in the introduction.

Positioning the nails Place the graph paper over the right side of the board, holding the corners in place with drawing pins. Hammer the nails in position through the paper, and remove the paper pattern carefully.

Threading the design Tie on with light blue thread at A1, A1 to B1, B1 to A2, A2 to B2 and so on until you reach A64 and tie off. Tie on again with turquoise thread at C1 and pass the thread down alternate sides of the nails on line C until you reach C64. Return in the same way along the next line of nails until all the nails between lines C and A are used and tie off. Tie on again with turquoise at H1 and wind round G1, F1 and E1 to

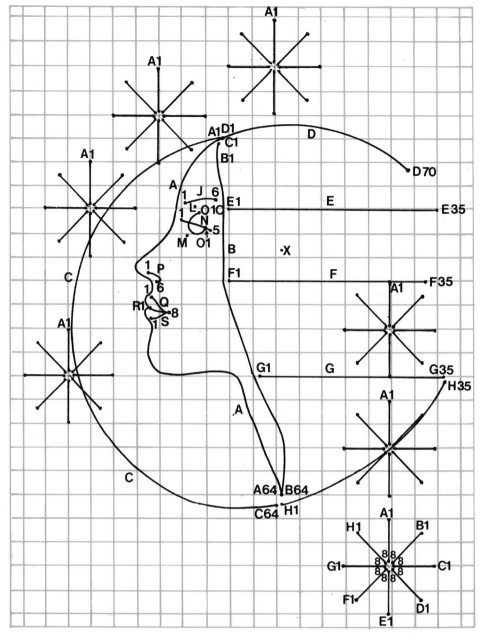

D1. From D1 pass the thread to D2 and then down to E1, F1, G1 and H1 winding the thread the other way round the nails. From H2 proceed in the same way until you reach D70 and tie off. Tie on again with dark blue at J1, J1 to J2, J2 to J3 to J6 and back to J1 and tie off. Also with dark blue tie on at P1 fill line P1-P6 in the same way and tie off. Tie on again in dark blue at Q1, Q1 to R1, R1 to S1, S1 to S2, S2 to R2, R2 to Q2, Q2 to Q3, Q3 to R3, R3 to S3 and so on until you reach R8 (which is also Q8 and S8) and tie off. Tie on again at N5 with turquoise

thread and pass the thread to L, L to N5, N5 to N1, N1 to N5, N5 to M, M to N5, N5 to N4 (which is also O1), O1 to O5, O5 to O2, O2 to O6, O6 to O3, O3 to O7, O7 to O4, O4 to O8, O8 to O5, O5 to O9, O9 to O6, O6 to O10 and tie off. To thread the stars tie on at any A8 and pass the thread to B4, B4 to B3, B3 to A7, A7 to B2, B2 to A6, A6 to B1, B1 to A5, A5 to B8, B8 to A4, A4 to B7, B7 to A3, A3 to B6, B6 to A2, A2 to B5, B5 to A1, A1 to B4, B4 to C5, C5 to B8 and repeat the sequence for BC etc., finally tying off at H4.

31
LIBRA

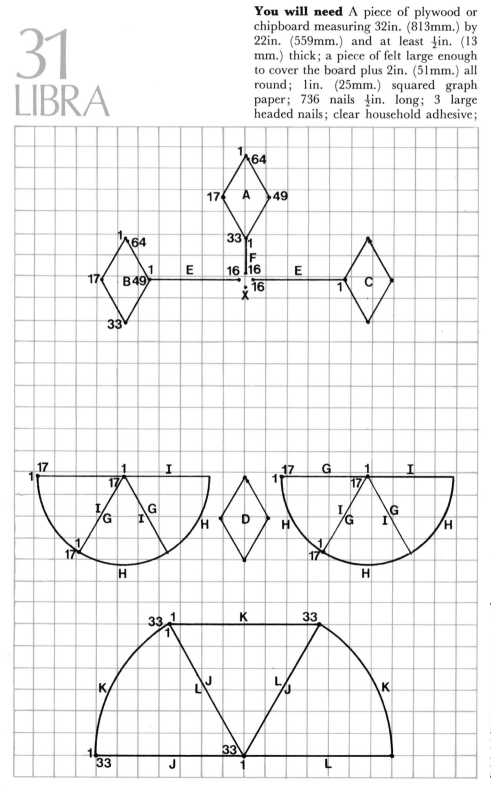

You will need A piece of plywood or chipboard measuring 32in. (813mm.) by 22in. (559mm.) and at least ½in. (13 mm.) thick; a piece of felt large enough to cover the board plus 2in. (51mm.) all round; 1in. (25mm.) squared graph paper; 736 nails ½in. long; 3 large headed nails; clear household adhesive; several balls of thread of different colours and 60 in. (1.52m.) of thicker gold thread.

The design On 1in. squared graph paper make an actual size plan from the diagram using a dot to represent each nail. On the four diamonds A-D the dots are very close to each other. For best results mark dots 1, 17, 33 and 49 and fill in the rest evenly making sure you have a total of 64 dots. Mark the rest of the dots as shown on the diagram using even spacing.

The board Make up the board as described in the introduction.

Positioning the nails Place the graph paper over the right side of the board, holding the corners in place with drawing pins. Hammer the nails in position through the paper using the three large nails at B33, C33 and X and then carefully remove the paper.

Threading the design Tie the thread to A1 and pass to A49, A49 to A33, A33 to A17, A17 to A2, A2 to A50, A50 to A34, A34 to A18, A18 to A3, A3 to A51, A51 to A35, A35 to A19, A19 to A4 and so on until you return to A1 and tie off. Repeat for Diamonds B C and D. Tie on again at E1 and pass the thread to F16, F16 to E2, E2 to F15, F15 to E3 and so on until you reach E16 and tie off. Repeat for the other side. Tie on again at G1 and pass the thread to H1, H1 to I1, I1 to G2, G2 to H2, H2 to I2, I2 to G3 and so on until you reach G17 and tie off. Repeat for the five identical sections. Tie on again J1 and pass the thread to K1, K1 to L1, L1 to J2, J2 to K2, K2 to L2, L2 to J3 and so on until you reach J33 and tie off. Repeat for the two identical sections. Tie on again at X and pass the thread down to D17, D17 to X, X to D16, D16 to X and so on until you reach D49. From D49 pass the thread down to K18, K18 to D48, D48 to K19, K19 to D47 and so on until you reach K33 and tie off. Tie on again at D17 and pass the thread to K16, continue as before and tie off at K1. K17 is not used. Finally tie on the thicker thread at B33, pass it right round the scale and tie again at B33. Repeat, tying on at C33.

32
SCORPIO

You will need A piece of plywood or chipboard measuring 40in. (1016mm.) by 26in. (660mm.) and at least ½in. (13mm.) thick; a piece of felt large enough to cover the board plus 2in. (51mm.) all round; 1in. (25mm.) squared graph paper; about 650 nails ½in. long; clear household adhesive and three reels of different coloured thread.

The design On 1in. squared graph paper make an actual size plan from the diagram using a dot to represent each nail. Mark in lines A1-A15, B1-B15 etc. spacing the dots regularly along each line.

The board Make up the board as described in the introduction.

Positioning the nails Place the graph paper over the right side of the board, holding the corners in place with drawing pins. Hammer the nails in position through the paper, and remove the paper pattern carefully.

Threading the design Tie the thread to A1 and pass to B1, B1 to A2, A2 to B2 and so on until you reach B15 and tie off. Tie on again at C1 and pass to D16, D16 to C2, C2 to D15 and so on until you reach D1. From D1 pass the thread to E1, E1 to D2, D2 to E2 and so on until you reach E16. From E16 take the thread to F1 and back to E15, E15 to F2, F2 to E14 and so on tying off at F16. Fill in sections F, G, H and I in the same way and repeat for the other side. Tie on again at I1 and pass to J16, J16 to I2, I2 to J15 and so on until you reach J1. From J1 pass the thread to K1, K1 to J2, J2 to K2 and so on until you reach K16 and tie off. Repeat for the other side. Tie on again at K1 and pass to L1, L1 to K2, K2 to L2 until you reach L16. From L16 take the thread on to complete the other side in the same way. Tie on again at M1 and pass the thread to N1, N1 to O1, O1 to M2, M2 to N2, N2 to O2 and so on until you reach O16. Now proceed to work the other four sections in the same way. Work triangle P,Q,R in the same way, leaving every other nail on line R free. Tie on again at P16 and pass to SS2, SS2 to P15, P15 to SS3 and so on until you reach P11. From P11 take the

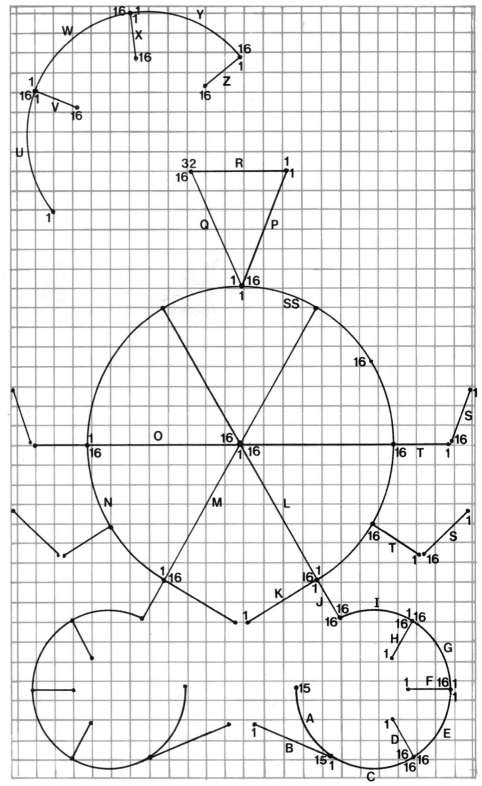

thread to P1, P1 to SS1, SS1 to P2, P2 to SS2 and so on until you reach SS16 and tie off. Repeat for the other side. Tie on again at S1 and pass the thread to T1, T1 to S2, S2 to T2 and so on tying off at T16. Repeat for the three identical sections. Tie on again at U1 and pass to

V1. Proceed as for section C,D,E,F,G,H. Tie on again at Z1 and pass the thread up to R16, R16 to Z2, Z2 to R15 and so on until you reach R1. From R1 return the thread to R32, R32 to Z1, Z1 to R31, R31 to Z2 and so on until you reach Z16 and tie off.

THE SIGNS OF THE ZODIAC

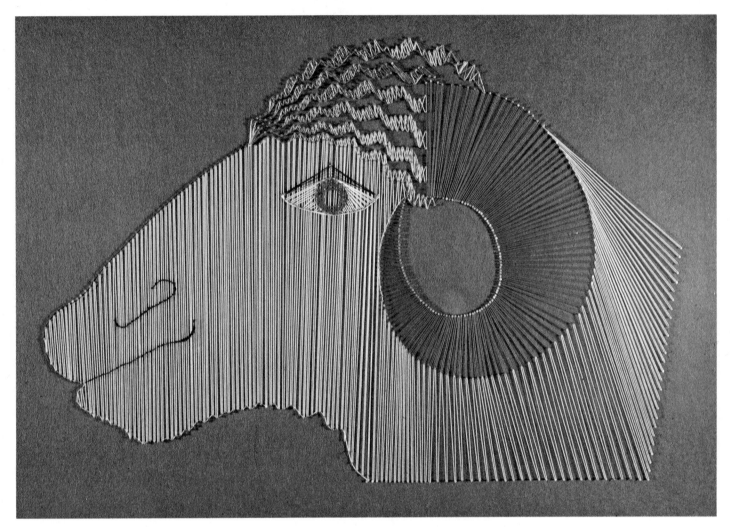

25
ARIES

26
TAURUS

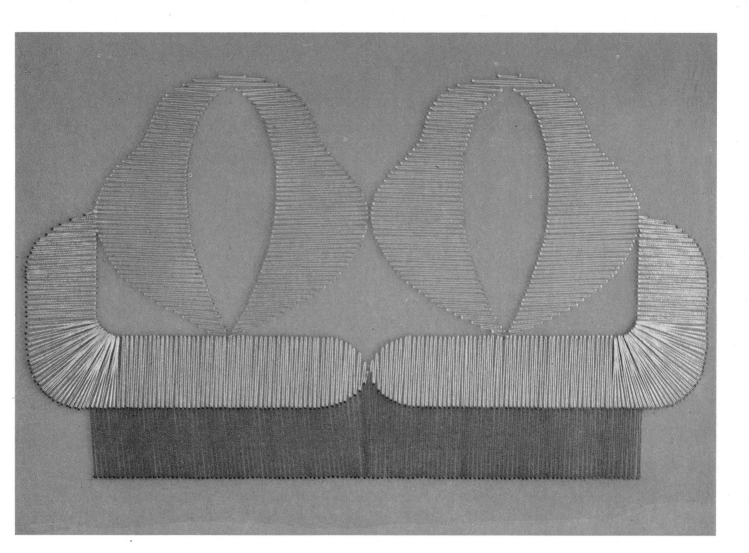

27
GEMINI

CANCER

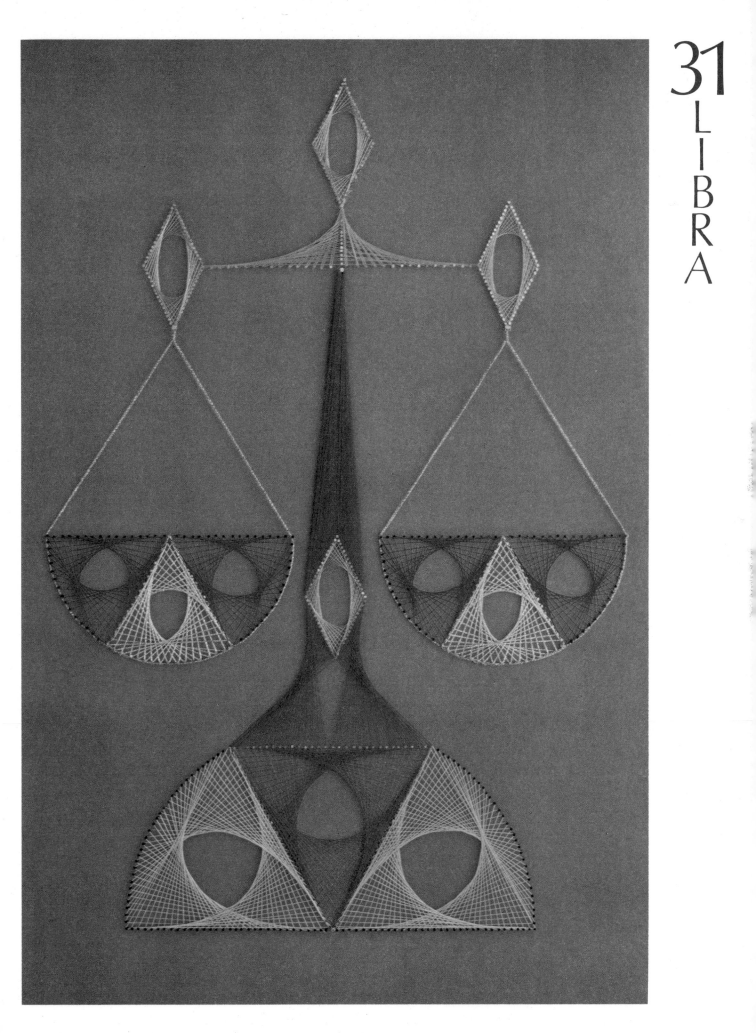

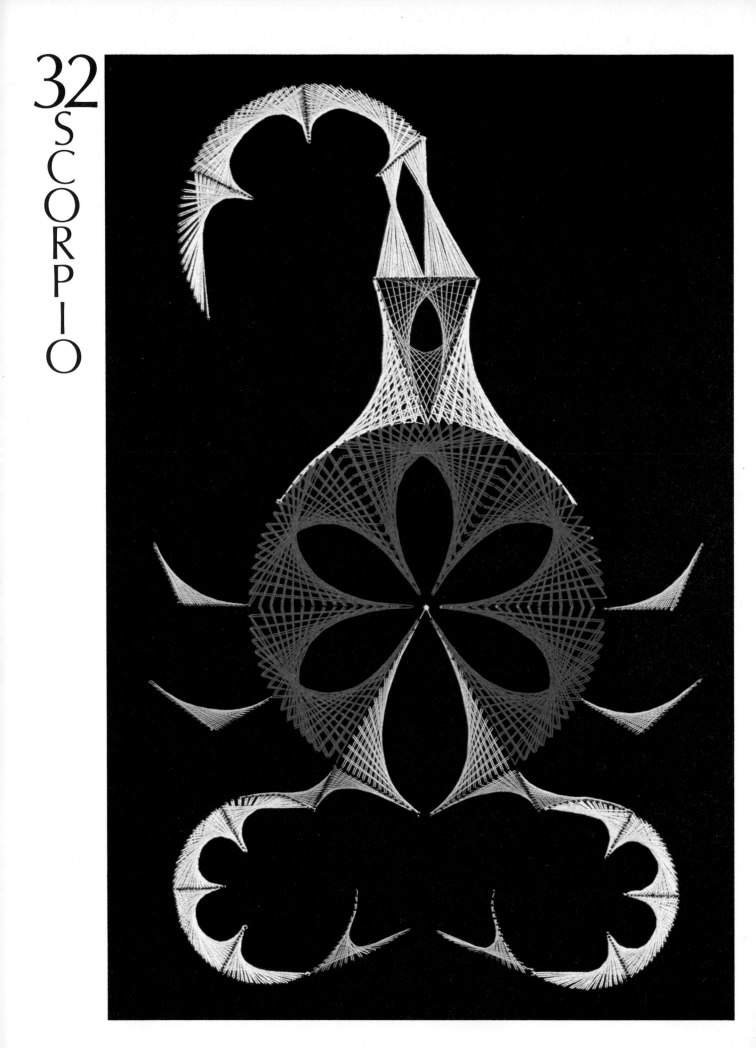

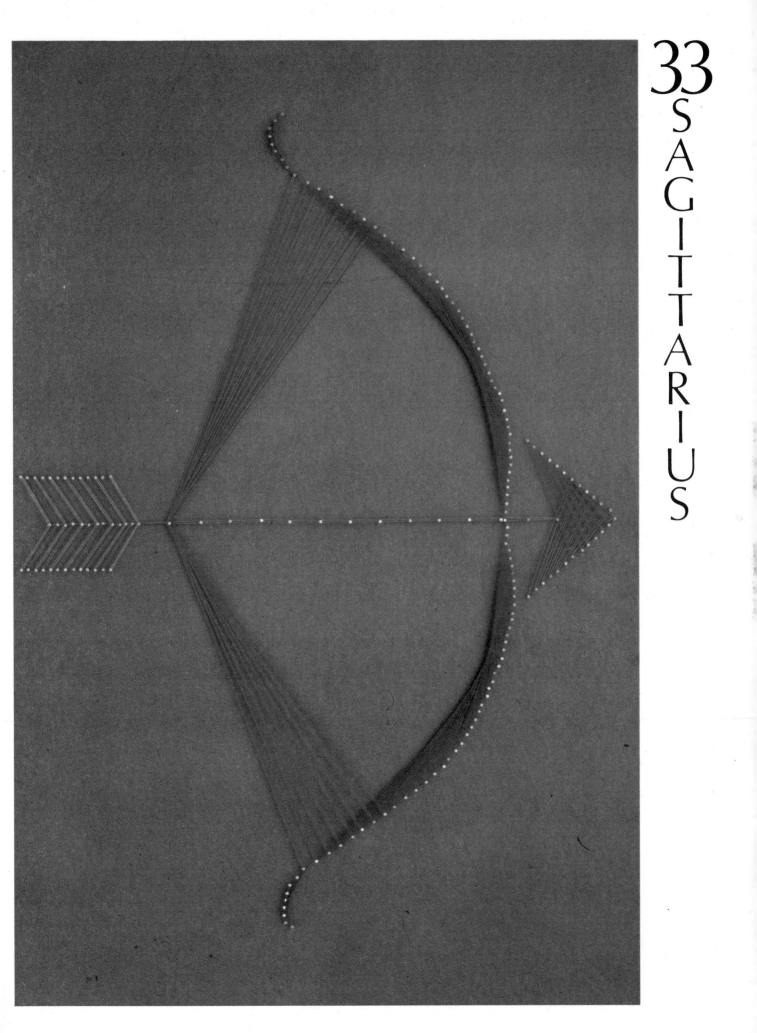

CAPRICORN

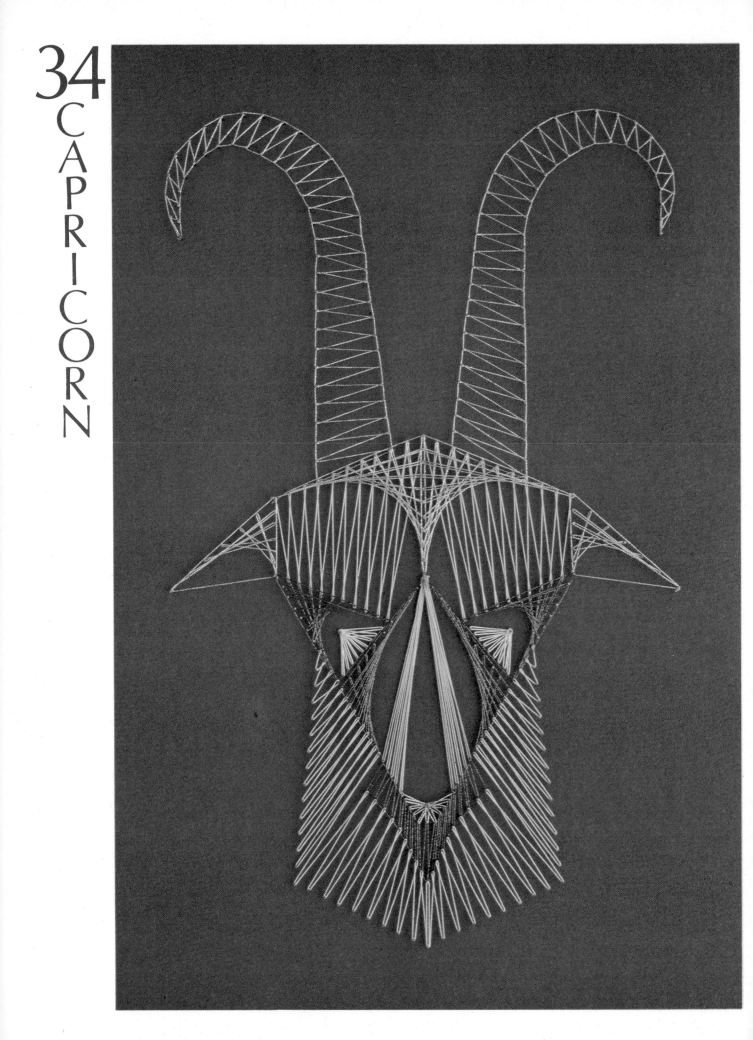

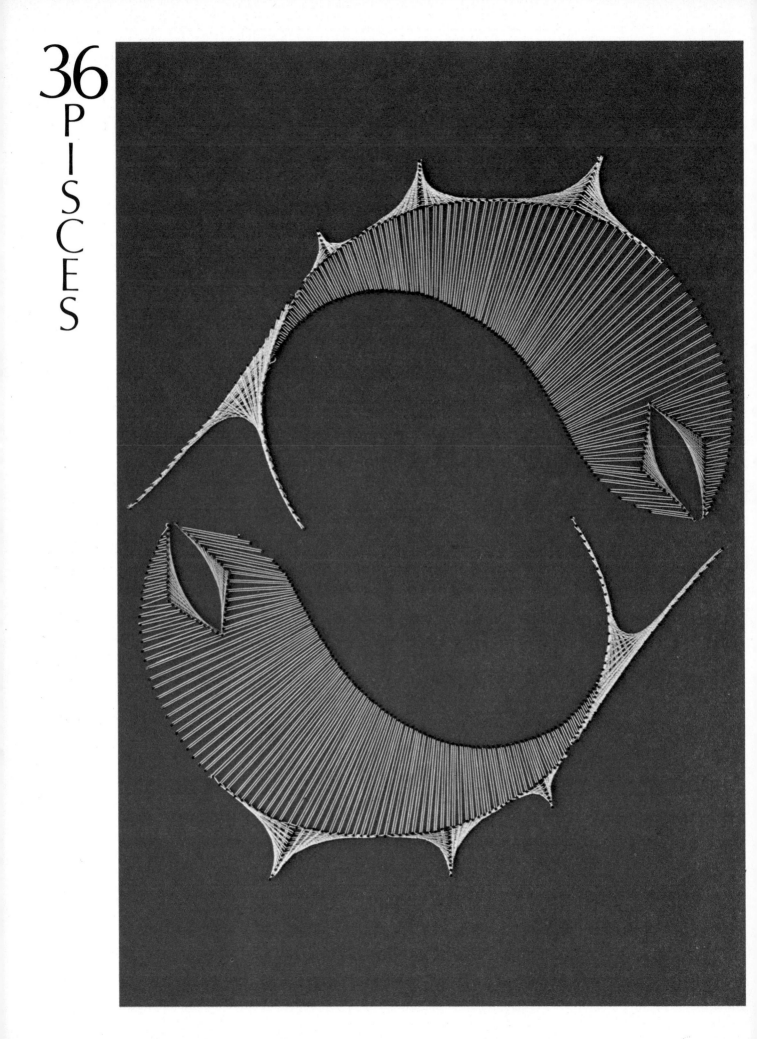

38
PEACOCK

39
DOUBLE
APOLLO

40
SPIDER'S
WEB

You will need A piece of plywood or chipboard measuring 32in. (813mm.) by 22in. (559mm.) and at least ½in. (13mm.) thick; a piece of felt large enough to cover the board plus 2in. (51mm.) around; 1in. (25mm.) squared graph paper with ¼in. (6mm.) subdivisions; 200 nails ½in. long; clear household adhesive and four different coloured reels of thread — we used tan, brown, red, and orange.

33
SAGITTARIUS

The design On 1in. squared graph paper make an actual size plan from the diagram, using a dot to represent each nail. Draw in lines A1-A55, B1-B55, C1-C43 and D1-D13, marking the dots wherever the ¼in. (6mm.) horizontals cross them. Draw in line E spacing dots 1-15 at 1in. intervals and dots 16-27 at ¼in. intervals. The dots on lines F and G are also at ¼in. intervals.

The board Make up the board as described in the introduction.

Positioning the nails Place the graph paper over the right side of the board, holding the corners in place with drawing pins. Hammer the nails in position through the paper, and remove the paper pattern carefully.

Threading the design Tie the tan thread to E1 and pass to E2, E2 to E3, E3 to E4 and so on until you reach E15. Return in the same way to E1 and tie off. Tie on again with red at E14 and pass to A9, A9 to E14, E14 to A10, A10 to E14, E14 to A11 and so on until you reach A16. From A16 return to E14 and pass the thread down to B9, B9 to E14, E14 to B10, B10 to E14 and so on until you reach B16. Return to E14 and tie off. Tie on again with brown at A9 and pass to A5, A5 to A8, A8 to A4, A4 to A7, A7 to A3, A3 to A6, A6 to A2, A2 to A5, A5 to A1. Repeat in reverse order till the thread is at A9, A9 to A31, A31 to A10, A10 to A32, A32 to A11 and so on until you reach A55 and tie off. Repeat for line B. Tie on again with red at D1 and pass to C7, C7 to D2, D2 to C8 and so on until you reach C12. From C12 pass the thread to C13 (which is also D13) and then to D7, D7 to C1, C1 to D8, D8 to C2, C2 to D9 and so on until you reach D12. Pass to C7 and tie off. Tie on again with orange at E15 and pass to F1, F1 to E15, E15 to G1, G1 to E15, E15 to E16, E16 to E17, E17 to F3, F3 to E17, E17 to G3, G3 to E17 and finish the line in this way tying off at E27. Tie on again in red at E16 and pass the thread to F2, F2 to E16, E16 to G2, G2 to E16, E16 to E15, E15 to E14, E14 to F4 and finish the line in this way tying off at E26.

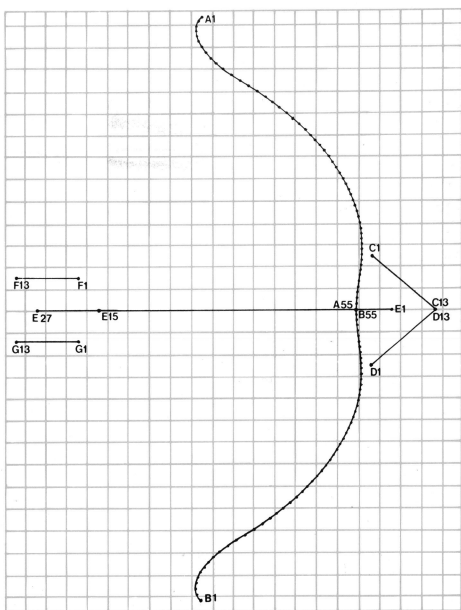

34
CAPRICORN

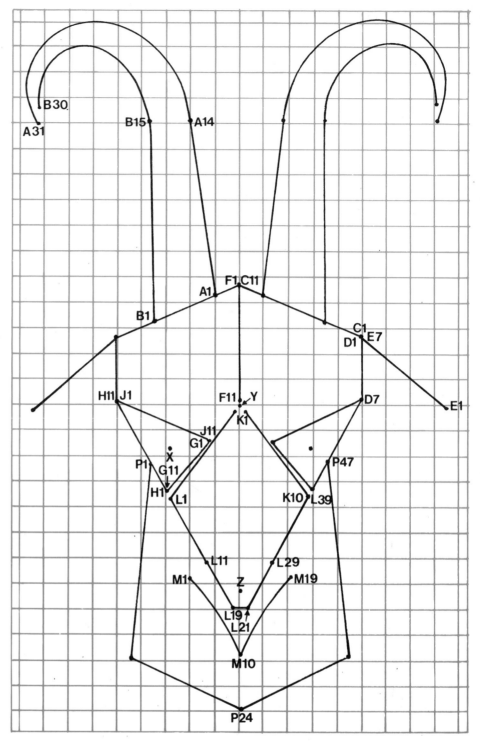

You will need A piece of plywood or chipboard measuring 32in. (813mm.) by 22in. (559mm.) and at least ½in. (13mm.) thick; a piece of felt large enough to cover the board plus 2in. (51mm.) all round; 1in. (25mm.) squared graph paper; 357 nails ½in. long; clear household adhesive and some blue, yellow and silver thread.

The design On 1in. squared graph paper make an actual size plan from the diagram using a dot to represent each nail. The dots along each line should be regularly spaced with the exception of lines A and B which have two different spacings. Space 14 dots regularly up to the points marked A14 and B15 and then fill in the remaining dots, also regularly, up to the ends of the lines.

The board Make up the board as described in the introduction.

Positioning the nails Place the graph paper over the right side of the board, holding the corners in place with drawing pins. Hammer the nails in position through the paper, and remove the paper pattern carefully.

Threading the design Tie the silver thread to A1 and pass to B1, B1 to B2, B2 to A1, A1 to A2, A2 to B2, B2 to B3, B3 to A2, A2 to A3, A3 to B3 and so on until you reach B30, B30 to A31, A31 to A30, A30 to A31 and tie off. Repeat for the other horn. Tie on again with yellow at C1 and pass to J2, J2 to C2, C2 to J3 and so on tying off at C11. Repeat for the other side. Tie on again with silver at C1 and pass to C11, C11 to F11, F11 to C10, C10 to F10 and so on tying off at C1. Repeat for the other side. Tie on again at D7 and pass to D1, D1 to E1, E1 to D7, D7 to E6, E6 to D6, D6 to E5 and so on tying off at E1. Repeat for the other side. Tie on again with blue at J11 and pass to H11, H11 to G11, G11 to J11, J11 to H10, H10 to J10, J10 to H9 and so on tying off at H1. Repeat for the other side. Tie on again with white at X and take to G2, G2 to X, X to G3 and so on until you reach X from G10 and tie off. Repeat for the other side. Tie on again

with blue at K1 and pass the thread to K10, K10 to L10, L10 to K9, K9 to L9 and so on tying off at K1. Repeat for the other side. Tie on again with yellow at Y and pass the thread to L11, L11 to Y, Y to L12 and so on until you reach Y from L15. Now pass the thread to L25, L25 to Y, Y to L26, L26 to Y and so on until you reach Y from L29 and tie off. Tie on again with blue at L29 and pass to L21,

L21 to L19, L19 to L11, L11 to M1, M1 to M10, M10 to M19, M19 to M29, L29 to M18, M18 to L28, L28 to M17 and so on tying off at M1. Tie on again with silver at L15 and pass the thread to Z, Z to L16, L16 to Z and so on until you reach Z from L25 and tie off. Tie on again with yellow at P1 and pass the thread to P2, P2 to H3, H3 to P3 and so on all the way round tying off at P47.

35
AQUARIUS

You will need A piece of plywood or chipboard measuring 32in. (813mm.) by 24in. (610mm.) and at least ½in. (13mm.) thick; a piece of felt large enough to cover the board plus 2in. (51mm.) all round; 1in. (25mm.) squared graph paper; 286 nails ½in. long; clear household adhesive and some gold, silver and blue thread.

The design On 1in. squared graph paper make an actual size plan from the diagram using a dot to represent each nail. The dots should be regularly spaced along each line.

The board Make up the board as described in the introduction.

Positioning the nails Place the graph paper over the right side of the board, holding the corners in place with drawing pins. Hammer the nails in position through the paper, and remove the paper pattern carefully.

Threading the design Tie the gold thread to X and pass it to A2, A2 to A3, A3 to X, X to A4, A4 to A5, A5 to X and so on tying off at A40. Tie on again at A1, A1 to A9, A9 to A17, A17 to A25, A25 to A33, A33 to A41 and tie off. Tie on again at A1 and wind round each nail to A41 and tie off. Tie on again with silver at B1 and pass to C1, C1 to B2, B2 to C2 and so on tying off at C21. Tie on again with blue at E9 and pass the thread to D1, D1 to E2, E2 to D2, D2 to E3 and so on until you reach E9 and tie off. Repeat for F, G (in silver), J, H (in blue), K, L (in silver), M, N (in silver) and O,P (in blue).

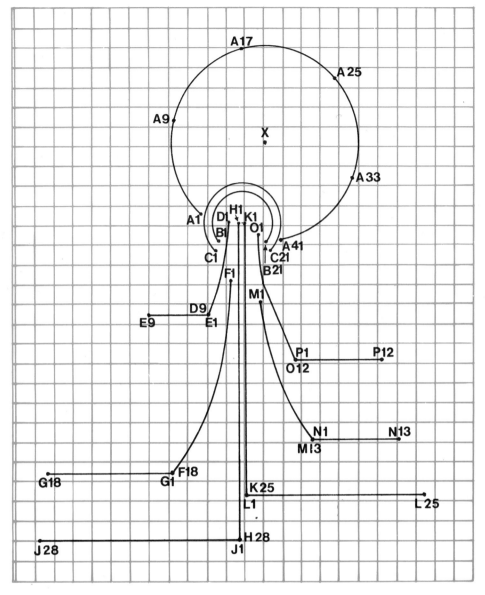

36
PISCES

You will need A piece of plywood or chipboard measuring 32in. (813mm.) by 22in. (559mm.) and at least ½in. (13mm.) thick; a piece of felt large enough to cover the board plus 2in. (51mm.) all round; 1in. (25mm.) squared graph paper; 575 ½in. nails; clear household adhesive and silver, gold and ice blue thread.

The design On 1in. squared graph paper make an actual size plan from the diagram using a dot to represent each nail. Mark lines A and B and mark 94 dots along line A spacing them regularly except for the last 10 which should be twice as far apart. Now put a ruler at point X and mark off 94 dots on line B by aligning the ruler with the dots on line A. Lines C, D and E have equal spacing.

The board Make up the board as described in the introduction.

Positioning the nails Place the graph paper over the right side of the board, holding the corners in place with drawing pins. Hammer the nails in position through the paper, and remove the paper pattern carefully.

Threading the design Tie on with ice blue at A1 and pass to B1, B1 to A2, A2 to B2 and so on until you reach the mouth. Now continue with line B only passing the thread round alternate nails on the mouth until you reach B94 and tie off. Tie on again at A94 and fill in the other side of the mouth in the same way. Tie on again with gold thread at C1 and pass to C15, C15 to C2, C2 to C16, C16 to C3 and so on until you reach C27. From C27 pass the thread to C41, C41 to C28 and so on until you reach C53 and tie off. Tie on again with silver thread at

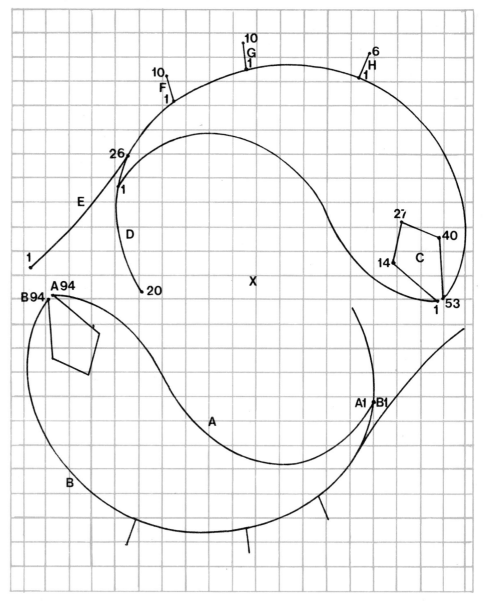

E1 and pass the thread to about B12, B12 to E2, E2 to B10, B10 to E3, E3 to B8, B8 to E4, E4 to B6, B6 to E5, E5 to B4, B4 to E6, E6 to B2, B2 to E7, E7 to D1, D1 to E8, E8 to D2 and so on until you reach D20 and tie off. Tie on again at Y, which is 11 nails along from the point where F meets B, and pass the

thread to F1, from F1 pass it to one nail in from Y, back to F2 and so on until you reach F10. From F10 pass the thread to the point 11 nails the other side of F and proceed in the same way tying off at F1. Repeat for G and H, but with H the points are *seven* nails on either side of the line.

37
OIL LAMP

You will need A piece of plywood or chipboard measuring 17½in. (444mm.) by 30in. (762mm.) and at least ½in. 13 mm.) thick; a piece of felt large enough to cover the board plus 2in. (51mm.) all round; 1in. (25mm.) squared graph paper; 621 panel pins; two large headed nails; clear household adhesive; a ball of gold thread and one of silver and a scrap of wood or card for the wick adjuster.

The design On 1in. squared graph paper make an actual size plan from the diagram, using a dot to represent each nail. Mark each line A1-A31, B1-B31 etc. as shown on the diagram spacing the dots evenly along each line.

The board Make up the board as described in the introduction.

Positioning the nails Place the graph paper over the right side of the board, holding the corners in place with drawing pins. Hammer the nails in position through the paper. At points X and Y use a large headed nail instead of a panel pin. Then carefully remove the graph paper — you may want to use the plan again for another picture.

Threading the design First thread the base and stem of the lamp. Tie the thread to A1 and pass round B1 to B2 (see diagram), B2 to A2, A2 to A3, A3 to B3, round the nail to B4, B4 to A4 etc. Continue in this sequence to B31 and tie off. Make sure that the thread passes the same side of the nail each time.

Tie the thread to C1 take to D1, D1 to D2, D2 to C2 then round C3 to D3 etc. Continue in this sequence to D31 and tie off.

Tie the thread to E1, pass round C1 to F1, F1 to A15, A15 to E2, E2 to C2, C2 to F2, F2 to A14. Continue in this way to A1 and tie off. To complete the base, tie on at F1, and take thread to A17, A17 to C31, C31 to F2, F2 to A18, A18 to C30, C30 to F3 etc. Finally tying off at C17.

The fuel container is threaded in ten individual sections. Tie the thread to any point G1 and take to H1, H1 to J1, J1 to G2, G2 to H2, H2 to J2, J2 to G3 etc. finally tying off at J15. Thread the other three sections GHJ in the same way. Tie the thread to any point marked K1 and take the thread to L1, L1 to M1, M1 to K2 etc. finally tying off at M15. Thread the five remaining sections in the same way.

To thread the collar, tie the thread

to N1 and take to O1, O1 to P1, P1 to Q1, Q1 to N2, N2 to O2 etc. tying off at Q7. Thread the other section marked NOPQ in the same way.

Tie the thread to R1 and take to S1, S1 to T1, T1 to U1, U1 to R2 etc. tying off at U7. Complete the other section of the collar in the same way.

For the globe, tie the thread to V1 pass round X to V2, round X to V3 etc.

tying off at V82 having engaged the thread round X each time.

Thread the funnel in the same way. Tie the thread to W1 and pass round Y to W2, round Y to W3 etc. tying off at W23. Place a spot of glue on each knot to make it more secure.

Finally trace off the outline for the wick adjuster and cut it out of card or wood and stick in position.

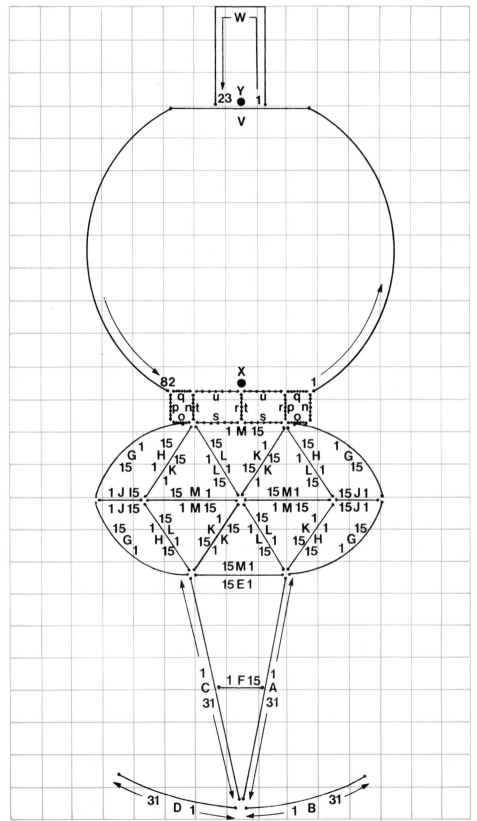

38
PEACOCK

You will need A piece of plywood or chipboard measuring 24in. (610mm.) by 24in. and at least ½in. (13mm.) thick; a small tin of matt black paint; a paint brush; 189 nails ¾in. (19mm.) long; 1in. (25mm.) squared graph paper; a ball of pink thread and some steel wire.
The design On 1in. squared graph paper make an actual size plan using a dot to represent each nail. Mark the lines A1-38 and B1-151, spacing the dots evenly along each line.
The board Paint the board with matt black paint and leave until quite dry.
Positioning the nails Place the graph paper over the right side of the board,

holding the corners in place with drawing pins. Hammer the nails in position through the paper and remove the paper pattern carefully.
Threading the design Tie the pink thread to A1 and pass to B1, B1 to A1 again, A1 to B2, B2 to A2, A2 to B3, B3 to A2 again, A2 to B4, B4 to A3, A3 to B5, B5 to A3 again, A3 to B6, B6 to A4 etc. In this way each A nail is used twice compared to each B nail. When you reach A38 pass the thread up to B76 on the left side and back to A38 on the right side and continue the same sequence as before until you reach A1 again and tie off. For a shimmering effect repeat the entire sequence with steel wire on top of the pink thread.

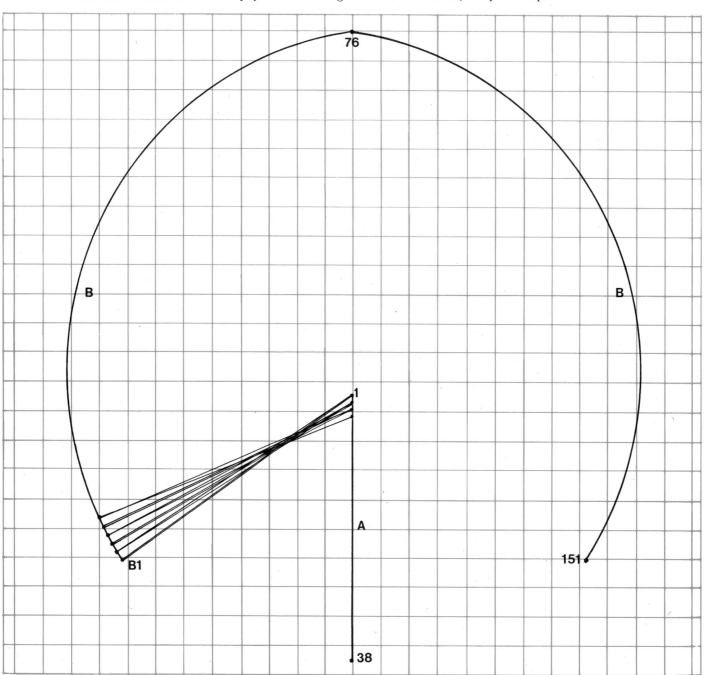

86

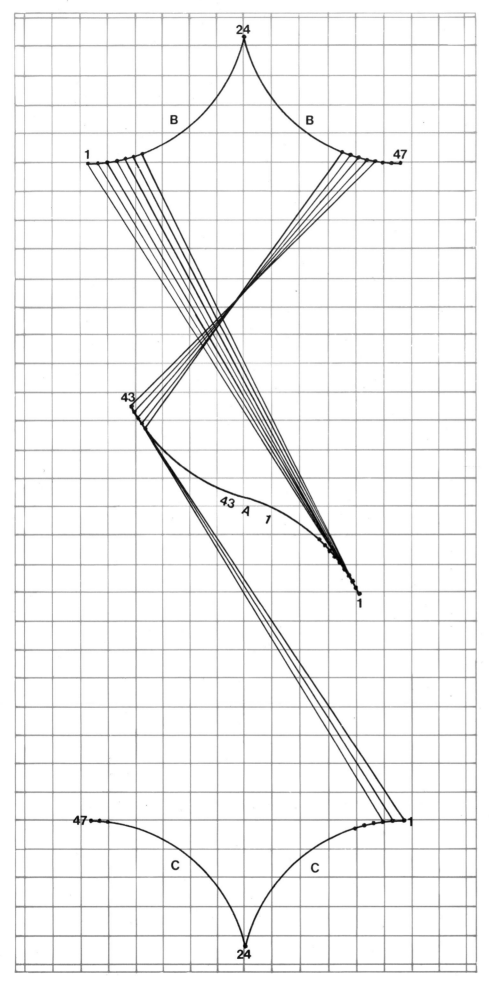

39
DOUBLE APOLLO

You will need A piece of plywood or chipboard measuring 33in. (837mm.) by 14in. (356mm.) and at least ½in. (13mm.) thick; a small tin of matt black paint; a paint brush; 177 nails ¾in. (19mm.) long; 1in. (25mm.) squared graph paper and one ball of gold thread and one of red.

The design On 1in. squared graph paper make an actual size plan using a dot to represent each nail. Mark each line A1-A43, B1-B47 etc. as shown on the diagram, and space the dots evenly along each line.

The board Paint the board with matt black paint and leave until quite dry.

Positioning the nails Place the graph paper over the right side of the board, holding the corners in place with drawing pins. Hammer the nails in position through the paper, and remove the paper pattern carefully.

Threading the design Tie the gold thread to A1 and pass to B1, B1 to A2, A2 to B2 etc. Continue until you reach A43 (leaving nails B45, 46 and 47 unused). Now pass from A43 to C1, C1 to A42, A42 to C2 and so on until you reach A1 and tie off (leaving nails C45, 46 and 47 unused). Tie the red thread to A43 and pass over the gold thread to B47, B47 to A42, A42 to B46 and continue in this sequence until you reach A1 (leaving B1, 2 and 3 with only gold thread). Now pass from A1 to C47, C47 to A2, A2 to C46 until you reach A43 and tie off (leaving C1, 2 and 3 with only gold thread).

SPIDER'S WEB

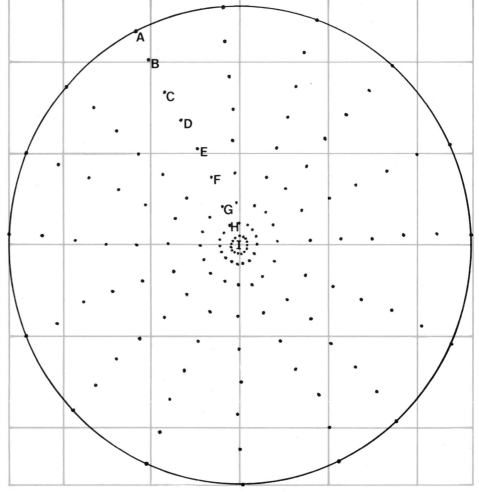

This design is an example of using pins and thread in a much less formal way. Once you have worked through these patterns you may like to experiment not only with formal designs but also with this kind of free approach.

You will need A piece of imitation bark (available from florists or pet stores) about 12in. (305mm.) by 9in. (229mm.); a box of dressmaking pins and some fine silver thread.

Positioning the nails Graph paper is really no help here, but using the diagram as a guide, put in nine circles of pins. Accuracy is no longer of the greatest importance.

Threading the design Tie on the thread at A and loop it round each pin in circle A and tie off. Work circles B-I in the same way, fastening off firmly each time. Tie on again at A and this time work the thread into the centre. Repeat from all the pins in circle A tying off each time in the centre.

Because of the great variety of nails available some very striking designs can be made by using nails alone. This section of the book deals exclusively with nail art. The technique involves using nails of differing lengths and thicknesses to build up a pattern or picture. Most finished nail works rely for their effect on the texture and shadow created by the use of different nails, rather than on colour. There is no reason, however, why pins with coloured heads should not be used to build up an unusual picture. Nails can also be used to form only part of a finished picture; for example small details of a design can be 'picked out' in nails against a painted background.

In nail art, there are no restrictions in the scope of a particular work but of course, it is sensible to keep to simple designs at first. The beauty of designing in nails is that a great many subsidiary patterns can be developed after the basic picture has been completed. A picture consisting mainly of lines and curves can easily be added to, for example by hammering in nails of a different size next to the original pattern. By doing this, considerable elaboration is possible. Nails do not *have* to be hammered into a board. They can easily be laid down flat and held with glue, to produce some striking effects.

There is no need to restrict yourself to producing works only on a flat board. Nails and wood are an excellent medium for three dimensional sculptures, and there are no hard and fast rules for producing them. However a sufficiently solid base will be required, such as a hefty chunk of timber, in good general condition. This piece of wood is referred to as the 'core'. The thickness of the timber depends on the height of the sculpture you have in mind. For instance, if the intended work is to be 12in. (305mm.) high the piece of timber will need to be at least 3in. (76mm.) thick, with a level base. It may be necessary to use a piece of plywood as an additional base for the sculpture. For heights above 12in. the thickness of the timber to be used should be increased proportionately.

Once you have a suitable piece of timber, the next step is to sort out the correct number and variety of nails to be used. It's a good idea to have on hand as many different varieties of nail as you can find. Different lengths, thicknesses, size of head as well as

different colour metals should all be used to add shape and interest to the design.

A nail sculpture totally relies for its effect on the versatility of shapes and textures achieved by closely grouped clusters of various kinds of nail. Remember to work the design all around the piece of timber rather than placing it too much in the centre. For added versatility, there is no reason why some of the nail heads should not be painted in different colours. For this job, a plastic-based acrylic paint should be used.

For knocking in nails in close clusters, use a light small-headed tack hammer.

The use of nails as an art form can be combined with other techniques. For instance, one very effective combination is an assortment of various types of nails and a variety of fabric remnants. Attractive and rustic collages can be made by cleverly balancing areas of nails with expanses of fabric.

It must be remembered, however, that where nails are to be used, a much stouter board will be required than is usually necessary for collages. The board must be thick enough to allow the nails to be hammered in firmly, and to a sufficient depth. If the nails are to be simply stuck down flat, the board must still be sturdy enough to bear the weight without buckling.

Having clearly marked the positions for the nails, begin to work the desired shapes. As with nail sculptures, it's a good idea to have as wide a variety of nails as possible. If the nails are to be hammered into the board use a light hammer. If the intended design is very imaginative and nails need to be inserted into the board to a number of different depths, first use a nail punch of the correct size.

By sticking down nails, interesting representations of cart wheels or sunrays can be achieved. A suitable glue is essential. Use a cellulose-based adhesive. When you first begin nail art it is best to stick to basic designs and techniques, but you will find you are able to tackle more complicated patterns as you become more expert.

In this book four splendid examples have been chosen to illustrate the technique of creating pictures with nails. Only basic materials have been used and by following the instructions outlined, you should be able to make similar works for yourself.

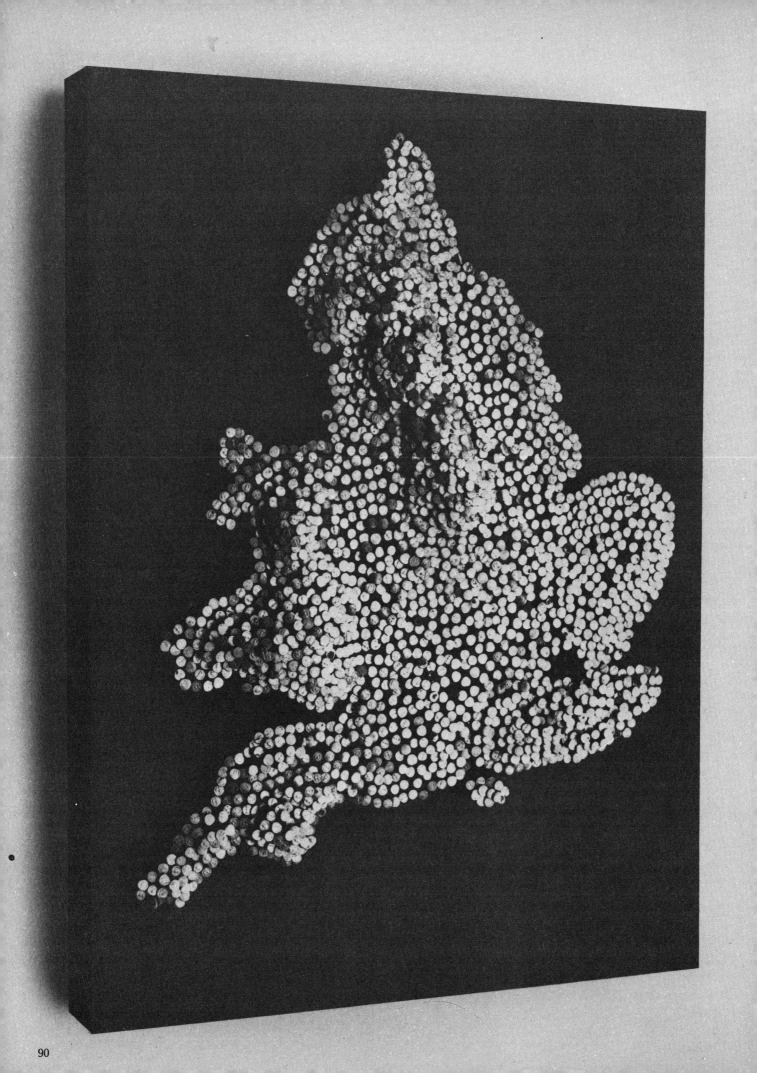

41 MAP OF ENGLAND

Maps offer excellent basic shapes for producing nail designs. Over a period of time a whole series of maps of various countries can be made to decorate the living room or study. This map of England and Wales was simply traced from a school atlas.

For this project, a solid board will be necessary. A great many nails are used in the work and because of this, a board that is too thin or soft will be likely to split. We used a piece of blockboard 12in. (305mm.) by 16in. (406mm.). Blockboard is an ideal material for the backing board as it is quite tough, but not too hard. The nails can be easily hammered in, yet are held firmly in place by the wood. A good alternative to blockboard is plywood. Be careful, however, to use an adequate thickness — ¾in. (9mm.) at least.

Before tracing the shape of the map, the board should be painted. Choose a paint that gives a tough and resilient finish. Highly recommended is a polyurethane based paint. It gives a finish that is virtually indestructible.

Once the paint has dried the outline of the map should be traced. Trace the map from an atlas taking care not to press too hard with the pencil. Having made a reasonably clear pencil outline, lay a piece of carbon paper — carbon side down — over the board. Now, lay the tracing over the carbon paper, and fix both to the board with masking tape.

At this point, it is important to make sure that the tracing of the map is laid absolutely straight on to the board. Having made sure that the tracing is straight, transfer the map outline to the board itself. For this, a soft leaded pencil will be necessary. Follow the outline of the map carefully. Take care not to press too hard with the pencil as there is a danger of tearing the original tracing as well as the carbon paper. Once the outline has been traced, a completely visible impression should be seen on the board itself.

It is now time to select the nails. In the example shown 1in. (25mm.) long flat headed nails have been chosen. There is no reason, however, why other nails should not be used. Beware of choosing nails with small heads for this project. In order to create the right visual impression they would need to be very tightly packed and hammering them into the board would be very tricky. Even with large headed nails this project is quite time consuming.

Having selected suitable nails for the work, hammer some all round the outline of the map taking care to get the spacing right. The success or failure of any nail picture is often decided by the spacing of the nails. The head of each nail in this picture just touches the head of the nail adjacent to it. If the nails are too widely spaced the finished picture will look sparse and bitty. Should the nails be too tightly packed the picture will look untidy and cluttered. Also, it will be difficult to hammer some of the nails into the board.

Once the nails have been hammered in all round the outline of the map fill in the 'body' of the work. The same nail spacing should be adopted throughout the work. Leave the major city area blank for the time being. Filling in the flat map is a fairly straightforward job, but to pick out the relief of the mountain ranges requires some attention. Look at the map in the atlas once more. Obviously it is not necessary to copy the shape and configuration of the mountain ranges absolutely accurately, but it's a good idea to try to achieve some approximate impression. This job can be made much eaiser if you acquire a nail punch, with the aid of this tool it is possible to sink the nails to any required depth into the board. If this is done properly, realistically undulating mountain ranges can be achieved.

Now is the time to pay attention to the gap left for the major city area. Select some of those pins with the plastic heads. These come in a variety of colours, of which the best for this work is red. These pins should be hammered into the board very gently — using a light hammer. Excellent for this work is one of those small metal hammers, sometimes used for breaking slabs of toffee. Knocking in the pins should be done gently so as to avoid bending them.

There is no reason why the ambitious beginner should not pick out several major cities in red and perhaps other geographical features or landmarks.

42 AQUARIUM

As mentioned earlier, it is possible to combine working with nails with other art forms. This aspect is well illustrated by this underwater scene. The background is painted on a piece of $\frac{3}{4}$in. (19mm.) blockboard. For this job, a plastic based paint like Acrylic is best. Painting the background does not require a great deal of artistic expertise — as achieving great realism is not the object of the exercise. It is the overall impression of the finished work that counts.

Once the paint has dried, it is time to decide on the positions for the fish. This being done, fish shapes can either be traced, or drawn freehand onto the board — using a soft leaded pencil.

Now, the nails should be hammered into the board to make up the bodies of the fishes. Small nails are best for this work, but there is no hard and fast rule regarding exactly what type of nail to use. This will depend, to a large extent, on the size of the picture in mind. In our example short ($\frac{3}{4}$in. or 18mm.), small headed nails are used to build up the bodies of the top two fishes, larger headed nails are used for

the bottom fish and the middle fish is made from coloured, plastic headed pins.

For a successful nail picture, it is not always necessary to hammer nails or pins into the board. Notice the top fish in this example. Its tail is formed by laying 1in. (25mm.) long nails flat down on to the board. The nails chosen for this have small heads. This makes sticking them down easier, and the resulting effect is more satisfactory. To stick any kind of nail onto a board a cellulose based adhesive should be used.

How to represent the fishes' eyes effectively presents a problem. It is possible to use a large headed nail — painting it to achieve the desired result. However, by far the best effect will be achieved if 'bull's eye' headed pins are employed for the job. These pins have plastic heads with a dark coloured centre. The surround is in a colour like white or yellow.

To achieve a more striking effect, some of the nails had to be painted after they had been hammered into the board. Oil paints could be used for this job, but in this example the artist used acrylic paint. This is a plastic based paint and is less expensive than oil paint. In addition it gives a tough and resilient finish and is less prone to fading.

After all the stages outlined above have been followed through, the nail picture will be complete. All that remains is to fit deal strip — of the same thickness as the board — all round the finished picture. The strip can either be glued or tacked to the four edges of the board. It will give a polished and professional look to the work.

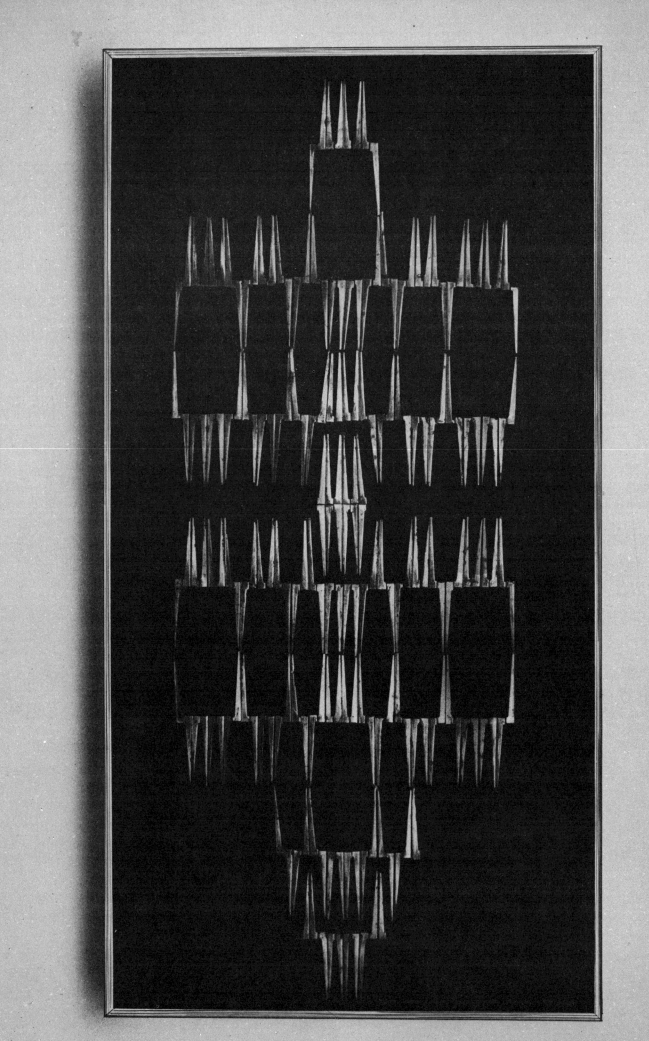

43
INCA
BREASTPLATE

As mentioned earlier nails do not have to be hammered into a board to produce some striking effects. This splendid piece consists entirely of blacksmith's nails stuck down onto a board to produce an angular but balanced pattern. Blacksmith's nails are squared and the head only protrudes from the shaft on one side. This shape makes them very easy to stick down. The nails chosen for this piece are 2in. (51mm.) long, although other sizes are often available.

If nails are only to be stuck and not hammered into a board, it is not necessary to use such a solid board. For this work a piece of chipboard measuring 24in. (610mm.) by 12in. (305mm.) and ½in. (13mm.) thick was used.

Before sticking the nails down, the board must be painted. Where chipboard is to be painted, the surface must first be prepared. This is done by giving the side of the board that is to be painted a coating of plastic filler like Polyfilla. Once this is done, the paint can more easily be applied as this surface will be smooth.

It is important to choose the correct paint. In the example shown here a polyurethane based black matt paint was used. With polyurethane paints there is no danger of accidentally scratching the surface when sticking down the nails. A matt paint was chosen because such a finish shows up the shine of the nails to its best advantage. Of course, the paint does not have to be black — but a dark colour is recommended.

While the paint is drying count out the exact number of nails necessary to complete the work. Following our example, or inventing a design of your own, begin sticking the nails to the board, one by one. A cellulose based adhesive should be used for this job. Use the adhesive from a tube rather than a can. This will make it easier to apply the small amount needed to stick down each nail.

Once all the nails have been stuck down in position, carefully clean off any adhesive that may have squeezed out from beneath the nails on to the board. A word on getting the nails in the right place. As each nail is stuck down, it is possible to slide it gently into its exact position before the adhesive sets.

Now, all that remains is to allow all the adhesive to set properly. Lay the finished picture flat on a table. This table should be in such a place that there is little chance of the work being disturbed. A good tip is to lay another board gently over the picture so that it rests on the nails. This will ensure that the glue adheres properly.

The picture is now complete. If any stubborn lumps of adhesive still remain visible, touch them out using what is left of the paint.

The finished work will look good anywhere in the home. The design shown in this book is highly reminiscent of the motifs found on ancient Inca breastplates and headdresses.

44
TALISMAN

This piece is rougher and more primitive than the others, but is no less striking for that. It too relies for its effect on nails being stuck down, rather than being hammered into a board.

Again, chipboard was chosen ($\frac{1}{2}$in. or 13mm. thick). The board is 24in. (610mm.) square. The board should be painted before sticking the nails down. In our example a maroon polyurethane based matt paint was chosen.

The nails making up the body of the picture are

$1\frac{1}{2}$in. (38mm.) long with small round heads. They are stuck to the board with a cellulose based adhesive. Notice that they are laid alternately — head to point. At the end of each row a longer nail is stuck down diagonally. The nails used for this job are 2in. (51mm.) long with small heads. It can be seen that the effect achieved is of squared curves. To further enhance this impression darker paint is used in the areas enclosed by the diagonal nails and the ends of each row. Also, it can be seen that at the outer edges of the picture, nails are laid in a fan-like pattern. The techniques involved in making this picture are exactly the same as those described for the last example.

For an added touch of professionalism, deal strip of the same thickness as the board can be fixed on all four sides.